This special, first edition copy of

WOMEN AND THEIR QUILTS

A WASHINGTON STATE CENTENNIAL TRIBUTE

by Nancyann Johanson Twelker
has been published by That Patchwork Place, Inc.
This edition is limited to one thousand
consecutively numbered volumes, of which this is
number 292 signed by the author.

Nancyann Johanson Twelker

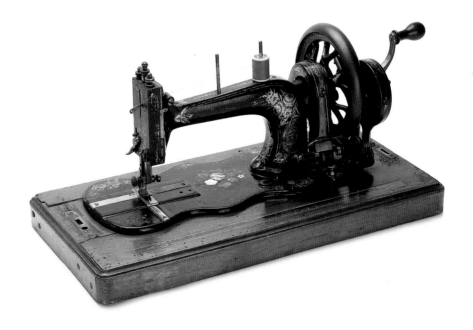

STEVE VENTO PHOTOGRAPHY

Victorian Bedroom, Governor's Mansion, Olympia Washington. This Crazy Quilt, with many United States bicentennial motifs, was presented to the Governor's Mansion in April of 1976 by the women of the state of Washington. The Washington State Extension Homemakers Council and the Olympia St. Peter Hospital Auxiliary coordinated this project. The blocks were made by women throughout the state. The South Sound Stitchery Guild set the blocks together.

WOMEN and Their QUILTS

A Washington State Centennial Tribute

BY NANCYANN JOHANSON TWELKER

FOREWORD BY CARTER HOUCK

Woman airing quilts and other bedding outside log cabin on Green Lake, Seattle, King County, Washington, c. 1890. (University of Washington Library Special Collections Neg. #UW593)

That Patchwork Place Inc., Bothell, WA 98041
© 1988 by Nancyann Johanson Twelker. All rights
    reserved
Printed in the United States of America
95 94 93 92 91 90 89   5 4 3 2 1

PHOTOGRAPHY: Skip Howard Photos except where
    noted.
DESIGN AND LAYOUT: Judy Petry
EDITING: Margaret Foster-Finan

LIBRARY OF CONGRESS CATALOGING-IN-PUBLICATION DATA

Twelker, Nancyann Johanson
    Women and their quilts.

    Bibliography: p.
    Includes index.
    1. Quilting--Washington (State)--History.
2. Quiltmakers--Washington (State)--History.
3. Washington (State)--Social life and customs.
I. Title.
TT835.T84 1988   746.9'7'09797   88-50425
ISBN 0-943574-52-8
ISBN 0-943574-51-X (pbk.)

WOMEN AND THEIR QUILTS:

A WASHINGTON STATE CENTENNIAL TRIBUTE
*is officially supported by the 1989
Washington Centennial Commission.*

OPENING EXHIBIT

Bellevue Art Museum
301 Bellevue Square
Bellevue, Washington 98004
January 14-February 21, 1989

This project is supported, in part, by a
grant from the Washington State Arts Commission.

WASHINGTON STATE ARTS COMMISSION

TRAVELING EXHIBIT

Fort Walla Walla Museum
Myra Road (between Rose Street and
Dallas Military Road)
April 28-May 14, 1989

West Coast Quilter's Conference
Sea-Tac Red Lion Inn
Seattle, WA
July 19-July 22, 1989

Washington State Quilter's Show
Convention Center
Spokane, WA
October 6-8, 1989

Washington State Capital Museum
211 West 21st Avenue
Olympia, WA
November 18, 1989-February 26, 1990

This book is the official exhibit catalog for
WOMEN AND THEIR QUILTS: A WASHINGTON STATE CENTENNIAL TRIBUTE.

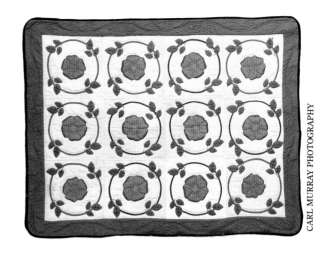

CARL MURRAY PHOTOGRAPHY

Rose Wreath Quilt, 38½" x 50", 1927. Made by Lulu B. McCurdy Johanson, age sixteen, Tacoma, Pierce County, Washington.

✿ This book is a loving tribute to the six generations of Washington State women in my family who have enjoyed all the needle arts and, in particular, quilting.

MY GREAT-GRANDMOTHERS:

1856–1940   *Nancy Tucker Stevens McCurdy*

My great-grandmother Nancy was a tailor who made beautifully stitched men's suits. When piecing quilts, she sat in a sewing rocker by the dining room window, and kept her needle and pins on the windowsill. She cut strips of leather from her old black shoe tops and fastened them around her finger under the quilt to protect it when quilting. For my birth, she made a pale yellow and blue cotton Ohio Star quilt, which I still have. She tended the farm and her two sons while my great-grandfather went to the Alaska Gold Rush for three years. She was small but sturdy and straight, and she stitched with determination.

1855–1926   *Susanna "Anna" Stedman Jones Carter*

After my great-grandfather was murdered, my great-grandmother took in sewing to support her two small daughters. She was an exquisite seamstress. She became head seamstress for Rhodes Brothers Department Store in Seattle. She made quilts and clothing until her arthritis made it too difficult to hold a needle. Her son-in-law made a special crochet hook to fit her arthritic hand so that she could crochet after she was bedridden.

MY GRANDMOTHERS:

1881–1954   *Lulu Verdinia Jones McCurdy*

My maternal grandmother twice lost her home and everything in it to fire. She referred to the fires by how many quilts she had lost. One fire was a sixteen-quilt fire. She made at least two quilts every winter, and all of us slept under "Ma's" quilts. She also made clothing, crocheted, embroidered, and shared her needle expertise with any of her many grandchildren who wanted to learn. My first quilting experience was on her quilting frame. I was so small, I sat on my knees on a chair to reach the quilt.

1873–1963   *Matilda Hansene Vanabo Johanson*

As a young widow with eight children, *Bestemor* journeyed to the United States from Norway in 1910 to homestead. She crocheted, knitted, embroidered, and learned to quilt by lamplight. Later, she helped the Lutheran Church make quilts for missions. She never sat down without a needle in her hand. She taught me the joy and the love of stitching.

MY MOTHER:

1911–   *Lulu Buren McCurdy Johanson*

Mother made her first quilt at the age of sixteen with scraps from her aunt's quilt. Parts of flour sacks were used for the background of the blocks. She is a perfectionist—her stitches were always small, straight, and precise—and a very talented lady, who made beautiful clothing for herself and her daughters. She taught my sister and me to take pride in our work.

MY DAUGHTER AND GRANDDAUGHTER, WHO WILL CONTINUE THE THREAD:

1951–   *Colleen Rebecca Twelker Earp*

My daughter's pioneer heritage has served her well. She is eager for knowledge and is very determined. She took a six-week basic patchwork class and made thirty-six blocks for her sampler quilt.

1971–   *Tina Marie Johns*

Tina loves to come to Grandma's house and pick out the quilt she is going to sleep under. She cross-stitches.

❧ CONTENTS ❧

FOREWORD

by Carter Houck

In the years between the two World Wars several excellent books on quilts and quilters were published. One of the best known of these was Ruth Finley's *Old Patchwork Quilts and the Women Who Made Them,* which appeared in 1929. At the time of the American Bicentennial in 1976, most people interested in quilts were still limited to this fine book and to Rose Kretsinger and Carrie Hall's *Romance of the Patchwork Quilt.* Little further research had been done. Indeed, there were few people who thought of quilts as much more than timeworn bed covers.

A combination of national pride raised by the bicentennial and female pride raised by the Women's Movement suddenly made quilting an art to be taken seriously. At first it was enough to determine the origins of patterns, the types of fabric, and the locale where a quilt might have been produced. It soon became obvious that there were specific quilters who put their mark as firmly on each quilt they made as Van Gogh did upon his paintings. Some quilters proudly signed their works, but many seemed to assume that the importance was in the work itself and not in the glory that would come after.

In this new wave of quilt research, an important function has been filled by various state projects. Some of these have been carried out by groups or guilds, some by a handful of people working with a museum or a university, and some few by dedicated individuals such as quilter/author Nancyann Johanson Twelker of Washington State. Each project has had a point of view, not always the same. One state, wishing to catalog and list for the future as many quilts as possible made in that state prior to the bicentennial year, finally had to call a halt at a documented list of ten thousand quilts. Washington State has only existed as a state since 1889 and as a territory for little more than thirty years before that, so many quilts made in the East were brought into the state in its early years. This fact certainly had an effect on the choices for documentation of Washington State quilts.

The features that set this book apart are the acknowledgment of quilts both old and new as worthy of inclusion and the fact that the maker—not just the owner—of every quilt is known and documented. The stories of many of the nineteenth-century quilters send little chills along the reader's spine. There is a feeling of reaching back and touching someone. As you examine the beautiful broderie perse quilt or the careful English piecing, you wonder how such treasures traveled unscathed over the long route to the West.

There must have been times when the only connection with a relatively comfortable life "back East" was the hour or so a day in which a woman could sit in her chair and piece or appliqué. The signed blocks of a Friendship Quilt may have been as close to a letter from friends as she ever had. For many of the descendants of the makers, the quilts were the best approximation of a family tree as they could put together. It is possible to feel the thrill as a current owner speaks, "The quiltmaker was my mother's mother's aunt, and I am named for her." She speaks not of a piece of silver or china purchased at a store, but of an almost living piece of the woman who made this treasure—a total reminder of the person she was and the taste she had.

As the families traveled West and as Washington State was settled, many of the women had a deep sense of dislocation, of being not only separated from their families but miles from their nearest neighbors. To be able to take the quilt made years ago by mother or aunt or sister and lay it on the bed in a new one-room house must have been comforting. We wonder whether they also envisioned the future, the family to come years later when life would be more civilized and houses more elegant. Did they piece new quilts out of necessity or were they, too, trying to leave a permanent record of themselves?

One hundred and thirty or forty years is not such a very long time, but the world today would not be recognizable to the women who journeyed to the West that long ago. Many of the families mentioned in this book went only part of the way, to Ohio or Nebraska, in the mid-nineteenth century. Their children or grandchildren completed the journey to the West Coast by the end of the century. But at that time there was little dependable communication and certainly no jets to return them to their families.

Even after the advent of better rail lines and a few automobiles, it was difficult to take large numbers of household possessions across the country. Once a family had traversed those hundreds of miles, there was little going back, little sending for what you'd left behind. One of the few treasures that could be justified by many women was a quilt. It was warm and useful along the way, did not take up much room, could not be broken, and was a thing of beauty in a bare new home.

It is possible that some families were so busy tilling the soil, building the house, getting the business started that they forgot about family. Older brothers and sisters left "back East" died, and the nieces and nephews stopped writing. Even family names became lost. In the past twelve years when Americans have become aware of the importance of family, of roots, of history, and have searched for long-lost cousins, the quilts that are signed, the few old torn letters, and anything telling a little bit about that dim past have grown in importance. The quilts made by a group and signed with many names can lead to weeks and months of patient tracing backward.

Each research project brings to light some remarkable women who have not even been remembered by their families for years and years. It is now not unusual to hear someone say, "I just found out that the quilter was my great-grandmother. I knew the quilt came down in the family but it took a lot of questions of a lot of people to find out who the maker was. She was also the first school teacher (or nurse or woman elected to office) in this town!" What a thrill, for both the owner of the quilt and the researcher!

We have better ways of keeping records today, better knowledge of what information should go along with a quilt or any artistic creation. It is sad to think of the many wonderful pieces of furniture, handsomely embroidered linens, exquisite wedding gowns that reside in museums and whose maker is unknown. Some families are better about oral history than others and can say with ease, "This table was made by my father." But sooner or later the oral stories reach a dead end, and the names are lost.

There are many unmarked graves across the country on the long route to the West. There is often more effort made to remember the soldier who fell in battle than the man or woman who lost life in the struggle to create a peaceful home, to build the schools, and to start the orchards. We should be grateful to the people who took time to fill in the lines on the family bible or to sign the quilt or the corner cabinet. Therein may lie the true record of progress!

Nancyann Johanson Twelker, in preparing *Women and Their Quilts: A Washington State Centennial Tribute,* spared no trouble and left no stone unturned in her search for the true origins of the quilts that intrigued and challenged her. The 1845 Robertson Quilt, for instance, took her on a long and sometimes frustrating telephone search across the country and into several states. Her clue was, of course, the Odd Fellows Hall depicted on the quilt. The story of the two Virginians who came to the West to make their home before the Civil War is one of perseverance and success, a model for the researcher, no doubt!

The author's organization and methods should stand as an example to others who wish to follow in her footsteps. She not only wrote initial letters to all of the museums and historical societies in Washington State, but had bulletins posted asking for help from anyone who read them. Guilds and quilt shows were very cooperative in notifying even the most casual passersby.

Then, of course, came the filing of material, the sorting of pictures, and the endless decision making. As the field narrowed down, a five-page questionnaire was prepared. The owner of each chosen quilt filled this out to the best of his or her ability. Then the real probing and research began! Slowly bits of lives and families emerged, and the quilts began to tell their stories!

As the years go on researchers will think of new ways to make quilts speak, to compile family histories, and to keep these records for those who come after. Meanings will become clearer. Why were there so many blue and white quilts in the last part of the nineteenth century? Why did some quiltmakers sign their work and others did not? More will be known about the wonderful patriotic and political quilts, as well as many other commemorative pieces that were certainly not made to be used on a bed. Were they all made for presentation or were they created in some outburst of zeal over a time or an event?

The stories will always be there, waiting for people like Nancyann Johanson Twelker, herself a fourth-generation quilter and a tireless researcher of quilts. The body of women's history will be much enriched by those who love quilts as well as those who made them and those who still make them. It is to be hoped that quilts like the ones pictured in this volume and the stories attached to them will be a source of pride to women for many years to come.

ACKNOWLEDGMENTS

Heartfelt thanks are extended to all who willingly shared their quilts, family histories, and photographs.

My research and documentation of the quilts was aided by the generous help of Kim Turner of the Seattle Public Library; Norman D. Gleason, Sovereign Grand Secretary, Sovereign Grand Lodge, of the Independent Order of Odd Fellows, Winston-Salem, South Carolina; the Yakima Valley Genealogy Society, Yakima, Washington; Verna Johns of the Lincoln County Historical Society, Davenport, Washington; and my friend Harry Branchaud, a member of the International Seal, Label and Cigar Band Society, San Leandro, California.

It would be impossible to thank adequately all of the other individuals who contributed time to *Women and Their Quilts: A Washington State Centennial Tribute.* Without their interest and support and that of the persons listed here, this project would not have been possible: Karoline Patterson Bresenhan, Marion Ray Reid, Rose Haldeman, Marguerite Knipe, Janet Lockhart, Joyce Pennington, Leila Martin, Sharon Yenter of In the Beginning—Quilts, Ann Stohl of Ann Louise Fabric and Folkart, Diane Coombs of Quilt with Ease, Ann Troianello and Glenna Brock of Washington State Quilt Heritage. And my gratitude to Al and David Twelker for supporting my commitment to this project.

CARL MURRAY PHOTOGRAPHY

Laura Ashley Washington State Pictorial, 72" x 72", 1985. Made by Wednesday Friendship Quilters. (Owned by Vivian Heimer, Seattle)

INTRODUCTION

Women and Their Quilts: A Washington State Centennial Tribute celebrates quilts and the women who have made artistic and cultural contributions to our state history and heritage through quiltmaking. In honoring this art and the women who have been and are presently engaged in it, this book encourages the preservation of quilts as "documents" of history and the preservation of quiltmaking as a unique folk art.

Traditionally, quiltmaking has been a practical and social activity, which has given women an unfettered outlet for their talents and a sense of shared community. That community could be as small as a single family, where quilts, as expressions of love, have marked significant family events—weddings, births, anniversaries—or as large as present-day guilds, fundraisers, or international exchanges. More recently, quilts are being recognized for their dual role—as works of art and as treasured bridges between the past and the present.

Many avenues have led me to the hundreds of marvelous quilts that make their home in Washington State. Quilt guilds, quilt shows, historical societies, museums, libraries, senior citizen centers, newsletters, and the files of Washington State Quilt Heritage have been some of my well-worn paths. In addition, on-going contacts with the quilting world through my teaching and various affiliations have also led me to some real "finds." My search for quilts has taken me to all corners of Washington State and has introduced me to many fine quilts and quilt owners, who have shared family histories, photographs, and pertinent information about their quilts.

Quiltowners who responded to my search for quilts were sent a five-page questionnaire. This questionnaire delved into the family history behind the quilt and its maker. Its purpose was to assure that the quilt and the quiltmaker could be documented. Documentation was my major criterion for selecting candidates for inclusion in this book. It was from this documentation that I began to narrow down my choices.

My other criterion was that the quilt had to live in this state, though it did not have to have been made in this state. I narrowed the selection even further by choosing a sampling of different types of quilts that would best represent the broad spectrum of quilts this state has to offer.

The main section of this book, Women and Their Quilts: A Historical Perspective, documents over a hundred and fifty years of quilts and quiltmakers. The amount of specific information on each quilt and its maker varies according to what descendants knew. In many cases families generously shared photographs and other memorabilia to supplement the histories.

The second section, Contemporary Women and Their Quilts, evolved as I was working on the first. It became apparent to me that in order to give a true picture of quiltmaking in this state, I would need to include present-day quiltmakers and their work. Washington State is alive with many quilt teachers, authors, lecturers, and fiber artists, who are known locally and nationally.

The third section, Collectors and Their Quilts, showcases a few of the major quilt collections and the women who put them together. Many of the quiltmakers in these collections are unknown, yet the collectors here are dedicated to preserving this visual legacy for future generations.

My own love for quilts and my interest in Washington State history has been rewarded by the many new friends I made while researching this book. I am especially happy that this search has kindled an interest in family genealogy and history in so many of quilt owners and families. I encourage each of you to thoroughly document your quilt(s) and its maker by recording all the information. In addition, actively support local and national registrations of quilts to record our quilt heritage.

Nancyann Johanson Twelker
Seattle, Washington
June 1988

Five-page questionnaire.

"The Patchwork Quilt," *1872, E. W. Perry,* Harper's Weekly.

A SAMPLER OF WASHINGTON STATE WOMEN

The legion of women who have contributed to the history, culture, and name of Washington State is nearly endless. If one were to make a quilt showing the greatness of these women, it would need to cover the 64,000-plus square miles of the state. The women who came here through wilderness and danger to carve out a better life were in many ways the reason we have a state. They nurtured their children and the land, fought alongside their husbands in times of danger, and took over businesses and farms when their husbands died. Yes, some failed, but never did they give up. This was home, a place to spread their quilts and watch their children grow.

fl. 1804–1806   *Sacajewea of the Shoshones*

Her date of birth is unknown, and her date of death is subject to debate. As an interpreter and a mother, she accompanied the Lewis and Clark Expedition across the United States. Her abilities as a peacemaker and her diplomacy during times of trouble helped to keep the expedition on course and helped the explorers achieve their goal.

1808–1847   *Narcissa Prentiss Whitman*

She was one of the first white women in the Northwest, and one of the first women to cross the Rocky Mountains. She and her husband Marcus Whitman established a mission in the area where the Snake River joins the Columbia River. They were tragically murdered during the massacre at the Whitman Mission in 1847.

1823–1906   *Mother Joseph (Sisters of Providence)*

Born Ester Pariseau in the Province of Quebec, Canada, Mother Joseph has been recognized as the first architect/designer in the Pacific Northwest. Building hospitals for the Catholic Mission and creating the Sisters of Providence kept her busy. She is honored by a statue located in Statuary Hall, Washington, D.C.

1834–1915   *Abigail Scott Duniway*

She arrived in Oregon Territory in the early 1850s. There, she wrote her novel, *Captain Gray's Company* or *Crossing the Plains and Living in Oregon*, published in 1859. As an advocate for women's rights, she became a driving force in the Northwest. She lived to see women achieve the right to vote in Washington State.

1849–1934   *Mrs. Ollie H. Ryther ("Mother")*

In 1883 she established the Ryther Home for homeless children in Seattle. She watched it grow for nearly fifty years. Her care benefited thousands of children. After heading the organization, she retired in the late 1920s.

1853–1918   *Emily Inez Denny*

She was one of the first white children born in Seattle. Her history of the pioneers, *Blazing the Way,* was published in 1909, the year of the A. Y. P. Exposition in Seattle.

1861–1925   *Alice Harriman Browne*

She was an author and the first woman publisher in the state.

1862–1940   *Ella (Rhoads) Higginson*

She came West in a Conestoga wagon. She became Washington's first poet laureate and one of the first women in Washington to achieve national recognition, this for her book, *Alaska, the Great Country,* published in 1908.

1866–1953   *Frances C. (Mrs.) Axtell*

She was the first woman in Washington to be elected to the state legislature (1912) and to be appointed to a presidential commission—Chairman of the U.S. Employees' Compensation Commission—which fixed wages for women in industry.

1868–1943   *Bertha Knight Landes*

She was the first woman to be elected mayor of a large city. She was Seattle's mayor in 1924.

fl. 1875   *Mrs. A. H. H. Stuart*

She was Chairman of the Board of Immigration for Washington Territory in the 1870s. Her book, *Washington Territory: Its Soil, Climate, Productions and General Resources,* was published in 1875.

1876–1956   *Nellie Centennial Cornish*

She came to Seattle in 1900, founded the Cornish School of Allied Arts in 1921, and remained its head until 1939. She believed that all of the arts were intricately interwoven, and that to master one, you must understand all.

1883–1972   Rhea Whitehead

She came to Washington in 1893. In 1908 she was named assistant prosecutor for King County. In 1914 she became the first woman judge in Washington.

1883–1976   Imogen Cunningham

She graduated from the University of Washington in 1907. Her contributions to the visual arts gained her international recognition. She was one of the great pioneers in photography as art.

1889–1972   Eva Greenslit Anderson

She earned her M.A. and Ph.D. at the University of Washington and was the second woman to be a regent for the university. Her biography of Chief Seattle was published in 1943.

1891–1975   Esther Shepard

She recognized the value of local folklore and legends. She wrote *Paul Bunyan* in 1924. She also wrote on the prose of Walt Whitman. She was a professor of English literature at Reed College and the University of Washington.

1893–1988   Florence Bean James

In the 1930s she and her husband established the first Seattle Repertory Theatre.

1896–1982   Erna Gunther

She came to Seattle in the 1920s. She was head of the Department of Anthropology at the University of Washington, and director of the Burke Museum from 1929–1962. She brought Northwest Coast Indian art to prominence here.

1899–1983   Viola Garfield

She earned her Ph.D. at Columbia University and

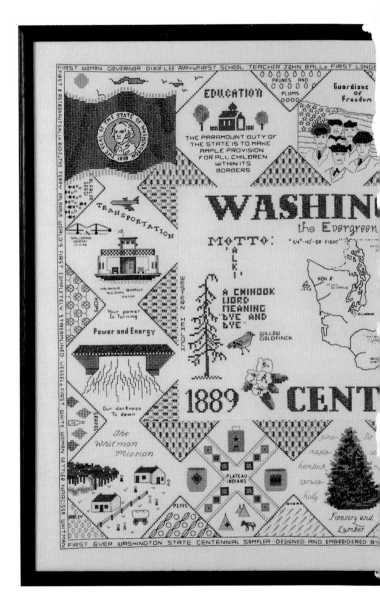

Washington State Centennial Sampler, designed and stitched by the Pacific Northwest Needle Arts Guild Sampler Study Group, Seattle.

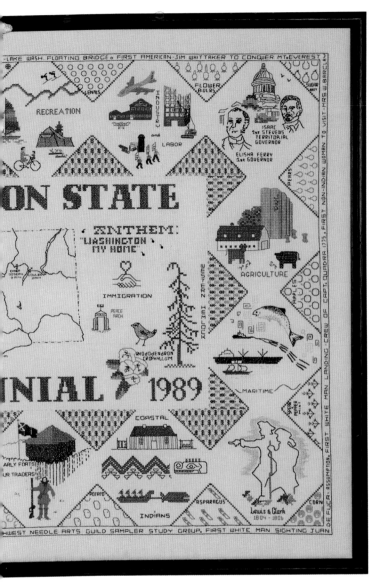

CARL MURRAY PHOTOGRAPHY

taught anthropology at the University of Washington. She wrote several books on Northwest Coast Indian art.

fl. 1935–1970   *Evangeline Starr*

She received her education in the Seattle Public schools and graduated from the University of Washington Law School. She was a superior court judge from 1935 until her retirement in 1970.

1908–1958   *Betty Bard Haskett MacDonald*

Her humorous narratives of life around the Puget Sound made us laugh. She wrote *The Egg and I, The Plague and I, Anybody Can Do Anything,* and *Onions in the Stew.* She also wrote the *Mrs. Piggle-Wiggle* books for children.

1913–1970   *Frances Farmer*

She was an actress of remarkable ability, whose radical thinking and alcohol problems shortened her career. Her films are still shown at festivals and on late-night television.

1914–1970   *Helene Madison*

A gifted swimmer, she set several records in swimming and won three gold medals in the 1932 Olympic Games.

1914–   *Dr. Dixy Lee Ray*

She was born in Tacoma and rose to prominence in the worldwide scientific community. She was Director of the Seattle Pacific Science Center 1963–1972; Chairman of the U.S. Atomic Energy Commission 1972–1975; Assistant Secretary of State, Bureau of Oceans, International Environment and Scientific Affairs U.S. Government 1975; Associate Professor of Zoology, University of Washington 1945–1976; and governor of Washington State 1976–1980.

Colfax. Wash.
1889

WOMEN and Q Their QUILTS

A Historical Perspective

Detail of Crazy Quilt, Colfax, Washington, 1889. (Collection of Rosalie Pfeifer, Kent) Sewing tools. (Collection of Nancyann Johanson Twelker, Seattle)

1833
ELIZA'S QUILT
106" x 107½"

ELIZA KAY BROWN, quiltmaker

Portrait of Eliza Kay Brown.

When Eliza Kay Brown made this elegant broderie perse quilt for her wedding of 1833, she probably had no idea that it would become her namesake for generations to come. But it is a fitting tribute to her handwork that the quilt came to bear her name and to be cherished by four more Elizas. It was great-great-granddaughter Eliza Leigh Mooers Anderson who brought Eliza's quilt to Washington State. Eliza Leigh also has Eliza Kay's four-poster mahogany bed, wardrobe, and dresser.

It is obvious from the exceptional condition of this appliquéd medallion quilt that the Elizas also passed down a tradition of preserving and caring for the quilt. It was used only occasionally, such as when an important guest spent the night, and then only as the top quilt on the bed—to be removed before sleeping.

Such care must have gone into the piecing and appliqué of the quilt as well, for Eliza Kay used imported chintz, which was quite costly in the early nineteenth century. A frugal quilter bought only a yard or so of this chintz and cut out the motifs from the fabric. She then arranged the motifs on the background fabric, which was stretched out in a frame. After basting or pasting the motifs in place, the quilter removed the fabric from the frame and appliquéd the motifs to the background. This type of appliqué is known as broderie perse. Notice that the appliquéd motifs are of a finer grade of chintz than the borders.

The borders measure 4½, 5½, and 7½ inches wide. In the 5½-inch-wide border, Eliza Kay quilted "EKB" on one side of the quilt and "1833" on the opposite side. She also used her ring to trace overlapping circles in one area for quilting. There are three sizes of the traditional "tea-cup" design quilted in different areas of this quilt. Outline quilting is used around the appliquéd motifs, and cross-hatch quilting is used in the center of the medallion and on the two chintz borders. The edge of the quilt is bound with a handloomed cotton tape of a simple weave. This kind of tape was often used for many projects around the house—bonnet ties, drawstrings, suspenders. It could have been woven in the home or store-bought.

A second Eliza quilt, a Rose of Sharon, was made to commemorate Eliza Leigh Mooers' birth. It was hand appliquéd and quilted by Eliza Potter Brown Leigh. Both their names and the date are embroidered on the foot of this second Eliza quilt. What a wonderful legacy to pass down from Eliza to Eliza.

Owned by Eliza Leigh Mooers Anderson.

c. 1835
WHIG ROSE (variation)
80″ x 80″
MARGARET MURPHY, quiltmaker

The Rose of Sharon or Whig Rose is said to have been the most popular pattern for bridal quilts. And because appliquéd quilts were usually "best" quilts and reserved for special people and occasions, they became ideal heirlooms to pass from generation to generation. It is likely that this is exactly what Margaret Murphy had in mind when she passed her bridal quilt on to her daughter Mary Murphy when Mary was wed. And Mary followed suit by giving it to her daughter, Kate, when she married Ambrose Collins of Carthage, Jefferson County, New York in 1889.

The quilt was destined to make its way West, for Ambrose, along with his brother Charles, had already sought his fortune in the Pacific Northwest a few years earlier. After being married in Copenhagen, Ambrose and Kate made the long trek back to Seattle, King County, Washington, where the brothers ran the Collins Brothers Undertaking parlor. They called Seattle their home for the rest of their lives. Kate died in Seattle in 1936. Because Kate had had no children, the quilt was left to her niece Frances McGovern Quinn, who in turn passed it on to her son (Margaret's great-great-grandson) and daughter-in-law Steve and Jackie Quinn of Seattle.

The family thinks that Margaret's family must have been Loyalist, as she appliquéd crowns in the 14-inch borders of her quilt, as well as love birds, weeping trees, leaves, and flowers. This charming border gives a folk art feeling to an otherwise elegant quilt. There are four 26-inch center blocks. Margaret quilted hearts on the large leaves in the center of each of these, as was customary on bridal quilts. She outline quilted around all the appliqués and quilted a diamond grid on the background. White thread was used for all the appliqué and quilting. The binding was cut on the straight of the grain. Cotton seeds are apparent in the batting. This quilt is in remarkable condition for having been used and at some time sent to the laundry; the laundry mark is on the back side of the upper left-hand corner.

In the early 1840s a rose pattern very similar to this one was the subject of a debate between the Democrats ("Democrat Rose") and the Whigs ("Whig Rose"). Each party wanted to name this pattern. When Democrat James Polk beat the Whig candidate Henry Clay for the presi-

Family gathering, 1911, Capital Hill, Seattle. Kate Murphy Collins is in the back row, third from the left.

dency, the pattern was named "Whig's Defeat." Now similar patterns are known by all three of these names.

From the Quinn family collection, Seattle.

CARL MURRAY PHOTOGRAPHY

c. 1845
ALBUM QUILT
72½" x 84"

MARTHA ANN JAMES, quiltmaker

It has taken close to a hundred and fifty years and many hands to complete the Album quilt Martha Ann James crafted and painstakingly stitched in the middle of the last century. There were the hands that signed the quilt—twenty-five of the signatures are men and women of Martha Ann's family—and the hands that quilted it a hundred years after the quilt top was completed. Martha Ann's granddaughter Effie Belle James (Pringle) and her great-granddaughter Helen Pringle Anderson started quilting it in the late 1940s, but it was not until the 1980s that Effie Belle's daughter (Martha Ann's great-granddaughter), Jean Pringle Swanson, had the quilting finished.

All the beautiful appliqué is sewn with tiny, uniform stitches, indicating that probably only Martha Ann appliquéd the thirty-eight 8½-inch blocks and the intricate half-block border.

Most of the 38 blocks have signatures. Some of the signatures are decorated with artwork done with a stencil or a very fine pen. The majority of the designs is done in the Pennsylvania German paper-cutting technique known as *scherenschnitte*. Original patterns were made by folding paper in quarters or eighths and cutting. This Album quilt has a padded medallion block that is 18 inches by 18⅝ inches. There is also a set of appliquéd carpenter's tools: a plier, a right angle, a saw, a ruler, an ax, and a plane. Set to the four corners of the medallion are blocks

Martha Ann James.

of appliqued shield-bodied eagles. This eagle design can be found on at least one other Pennsylvania quilt (see Kolter, Janet B. *Forget Me Not, A Gallery of Friendship and Album Quilts,* p. 44, pl. 40).

Martha Ann made a second quilt top; it has a prairie-point edge. The second quilt top remains unquilted, making it possible to appreciate both sides of Martha Ann's fine appliqué stitches. The family believes these tops were to be bride's quilts. They were never used, only brought out and aired occasionally.

Martha Ann James was born in West Chester, Chester County, Pennsylvania, September 22, 1827. She married Abraham James February 7, 1850. This Quaker couple settled in Fredonia, Chautaugua County, New York, a small town a couple of miles from Lake Erie and approximately forty miles north of the Pennsylvania–New York state line. They had six children.

According to the Abraham James family, Abraham loved nice surroundings. It was said that he was a very fine person, but somewhat of a gambler; he was "good pickins for a scheme to get rich fast." After a loss that wiped him out financially, he would just pick himself back up and make another fortune. Abraham died in 1862. Martha Ann enjoyed dressmaking and needlework until her death in 1902.

Owned by Jean Pringle Swanson, Seattle.

Album quilt top with prairie point edge.

c. 1847
FEATHERED STAR

81" x 93"

NANCY MARTIN DEARFIELD, quiltmaker

This red-and-white cotton quilt is beautifully pieced and quilted. It is made of red chintz and muslin and has 16 full-size, pieced Feathered Star blocks and 4 partial blocks, each of which are only ⅔ of the Feathered Star design. The quilt is bordered with a sawtooth border inside a solid chintz border. The individual sawtooth segments and top chintz borders are of a different chintz fabric, which suggests that there wasn't enough of the preferred red chintz to complete the design. Turkey red was a popular color at this time, probably because it was one of the most permanent dyes and resistant to fading. The large muslin areas between the Feathered Stars show Nancy's lavish and delicate quilting designs. These areas are heavily quilted with feathered wreaths, other circular designs, and clam shells.

Nancy Martin was born March 5, 1827, in southwestern Pennsylvania. When her betrothal to Orlander Stephens Dearfield of nearby Pleasants County, West Virginia, was announced, she began this magnificent Feathered Star quilt for her bridal quilt. It was common for young women to invest a lot of time in their bridal quilts, which would serve as a showcase for their finest stitches.

Nancy and Orlander lived in Pleasants County, where they had three sons: Oliver in 1861, Orlander in 1863, and William in 1868. After the death of her husband, Nancy went to live with her middle son, Orlander, and his wife Edith. The family moved West in the early 1900s to Beaver City, Furnas County, Nebraska, where Orlander and Edith's daughter Elizabeth was born. In 1913 they continued their westward trek to Twin Falls, Idaho. Nancy died September 6, 1914, her son Orlander died August 16, 1915.

Nancy passed her Feathered Star quilt on to her granddaughter Elizabeth. Elizabeth Dearfield moved to Seattle, King County, Washington, and was employed as a draftsman at Boeing. She greatly appreciated the precision and mathematical accuracy of her grandmother's quilt. Elizabeth never married.

In 1985 when Elizabeth was moved to a nursing home, all of her treasures were sold. Quilt collector Nancy J. Martin attended the sale and purchased the Feathered Star quilt. She then visited Elizabeth in the nursing home to gather Elizabeth's family history. Imagine her surprise when she learned that the quilt was made by someone with the same name. Nancy J. Martin returned to the sale and bought the Dearfield family bible and more of Nancy Martin Dearfield's personal belongings. However, Elizabeth became the real treasure. Nancy and her quilting friends "adopted" her. They visited her in the nursing home, they took her to quilt meetings, and they made Elizabeth the first honorary member of Quilters Anonymous. Elizabeth spent her final days feeling the warm fellowship of quilters.

Collection of Nancy J. Martin, Woodinville.

CARL MURRAY PHOTOGRAPHY

Feathered Star quilt with Dearfield family bible.

CARL MURRAY PHOTOGRAPHY

1848
POINSETTIA (variation)
92" x 96"
RUTH M. KNOX ALLEN, quiltmaker

Ruth M. Knox was seventeen years old when she made this red and green quilt. The color combination used here—solid red cotton and green calico cotton on a white top with a plain backing—was very popular in the mid-1800s. Close examination reveals that two women may have appliquéd it. Perhaps Ruth's mother helped her. This marvelous handmade quilt is a delight to study. The more you look at it, the more you see. It has nine 18-inch blocks set on the diagonal with alternating plain blocks. Three of the 8-inch borders have tear-shaped leaves, and the fourth has mostly diamond-shaped leaves. The red flower centers have 10 to 13 stamens, and the berries are different sizes, measuring from ½ to 1 inch each and 14 to 26 berries per stem. The beautiful quilting appears to be one person's stitching. The borders are quilted with a ⅜-inch grid, and the rest of the quilt is quilted with a larger double crosshatch design. There is an applied muslin bias binding.

Ruth was born March 19, 1831. Her father was a neighbor and very good friend of Abraham Lincoln's family. Ruth was married February 15, 1864, in Springfield, Illinois, to Louis V. Allen, who was born in 1841. Louis was a first lieutenant in the Union Army and fought under General William Sherman. Ruth and Louis had one child Estella Allen who was born April 17, 1871, in Dan-

Ruth M. Knox Allen. (Courtesy of the Lincoln County Historical Society, Davenport)

ville, Vermillion County, Illinois. In 1877 they moved West to Salem, Marion County, Oregon; in 1879 they went on to Waitsburg, Walla Walla County, Washington Territory; and in 1880 they settled in Harrington, Lincoln County, Washington Territory, where they farmed about five miles southwest of town. Louis was county commissioner for five years and a member of the G. A. R. (Grand Army of the Republic), an organization for Civil War veterans. When Ruth and Louis retired, they moved to Davenport, Washington, where they built a brick home. The house later became their daughter and her husband's family home. When Ruth died, Louis took her body to Springfield to be buried in the family plot.

Estella married J. E. Howard, who served overseas with the Red Cross during World War I. He was a representative to the state legislature and served as the Lincoln County auditor. In 1917 Estella was the first woman to hold an office in Lincoln County. She served two and a half terms as county auditor. Their only child Ruth Howard was born in Davenport in 1903. Ruth attended Cheney Normal School. She worked for the Washington Water Power Company in Davenport and for the Bureau of Reclamation in Ephrata. Ruth married Herbert A. Reard, an orchardist from Ephrata in 1930. They had no children. When Ruth died June 24, 1975, her grandmother's beautiful applique quilt came to live in the Lincoln County Historical Society Museum in Davenport.

Photographs and quilt courtesy of the Lincoln County Historical Society, Davenport.

Inside the Allen home (note scissors hanging on wall). Left to right: Ruth Knox Allen, Estella Allen, unknown, Louis Allen. (Courtesy of the Lincoln County Historical Society, Davenport)

c. 1850
MOSAIC
80″ x 83″
ELEANORE FINK ROBINSON, quiltmaker

❧ Eleanore Fink made this quilt for her hope chest. It is hand pieced using one of the oldest forms of patchwork, English paper piecing. In English paper piecing the hexagons are formed over paper templates. The fabrics are early nineteenth-century cottons. One color in the red print center has deteriorated allowing the cotton batting to peek through the fabric.

Eleanore quilted this quilt in an unusual but elegant manner. She quilted two, large feathered plumes, which arc gracefully toward the center of the quilt, thus leaving two half-moon areas on either side of the quilt. In each of these areas, she quilted a feathered circle. Inside the feathered circle and around the border of the quilt, she quilted straight lines every ¼ inch. In the remaining central portion of the quilt, she quilted diagonal lines every ½ inch. Eleanore bound this quilt with fabric cut on the straight of the grain. Her name is signed in India ink on the front edge of the quilt in two places.

Eleanore, who was born in 1818 in Washington, Washington County, Pennsylvania, took the quilt with her when she married John Goodno Robinson, December 6, 1853, in Carroll County, Ohio. Eleanore and John spent their lives on a farm near Bloomington, Monroe County, Indiana, until 1890, when they moved into town. They had four children: Frances, James, Elizabeth, and Albert. Eleanore died in 1891.

At least two of Eleanore and John's children heeded the call of the West. James Easton Robinson headed West

Left to right: John G., Frances, Eleanore Fink Robinson, Ella, James E. Robinson. (Courtesy of the Lincoln County Historical Society, Davenport)

in 1882 to seek a better climate, new opportunities, and in part, to escape from the strict Presbyterianism of his family. He homesteaded in Moscow, Lincoln County, Washington, which he later renamed Bluestem after the principal type of wheat grown there. James farmed and worked as a carpenter for the Northern Pacific Railroad. Both he and his wife Caroline Mecklenburg Robinson lived out their lives in Lincoln County. James' oldest sister, Frances, came to live in Washington State also. Frances taught school and lived in town with James and Caroline's children during the winter months. Eleanore gave her quilt to Frances, who passed it on to her niece Verna Robinson Welch of Walla Walla, Walla Walla County, Washington. Mrs. Welch gave the quilt to her nephew (Eleanore's great-grandson) James Robinson Teel and his wife Betty Jo of Davenport, Lincoln County, Washington.

Collection of Mr. and Mrs. James Teel, Davenport.

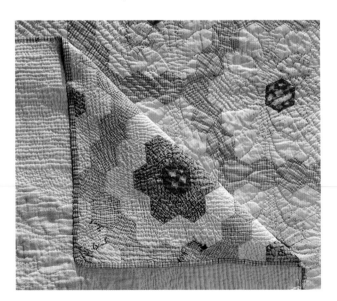

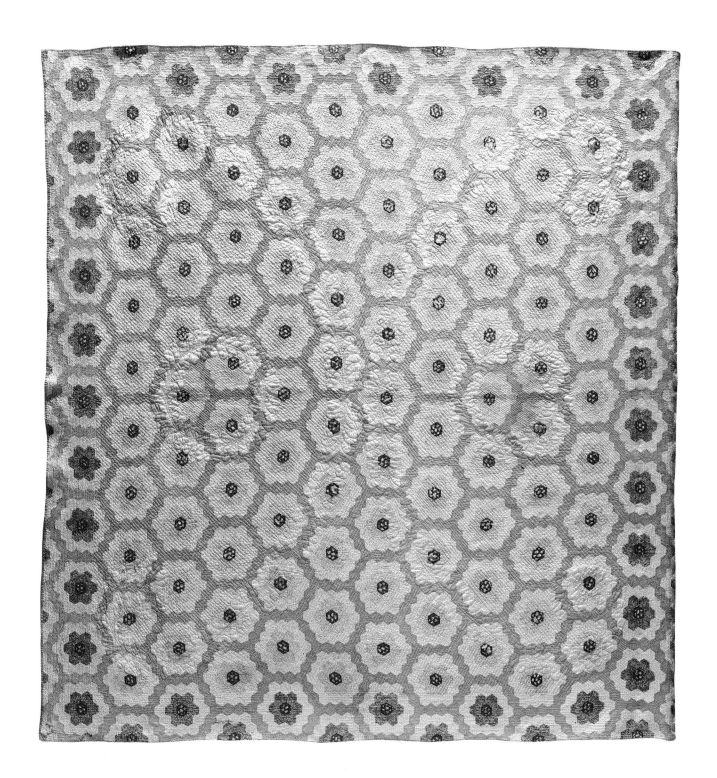

c. 1850
THE ROBERTSON QUILT

96″ x 101″

REBEKAHS OF I.O.O.F. LODGE NO. 1, BALTIMORE, quiltmakers

This stunning appliquéd medallion quilt is a significant presentation quilt. It was made by Mary Jane Pierre Robertson's Rebekah Lodge and presented to her when she left Baltimore, Maryland, for the West. The quilt has lived in Washington State since the mid-1850s.

In the center medallion is a replica of the first Odd Fellows Hall in America, Gay Street, Baltimore, Maryland. Odd Fellow and Rebekah symbols surround the appliqué of the hall, which is framed by a wreath of laurel leaves. Each symbol has its own meaning: heart and hand means that greetings should be of the heart as well as of the hand ("with pure hearts and clean hands"); the serpent is a symbol of wisdom; the scale and sword mean justice; the beehive stands for industry; the dove means innocence and harmlessness. Not all of the symbols are contained within the wreath: the moon and seven-pointed stars, the earth, the beehive, and the staff and serpent are appliquéd in the corners of this 31-inch by 33-inch medallion block. The remaining 32 unsigned blocks are of three designs: a moss rose and lily, strawberries with leaves and stems, and a branch of cherries. The rose, lily, strawberries, and cherries are padded. The block size

varies, about 16 inches by 16 inches. The workmanship varies from block to block. The quilting outlines each appliqué, and the background is quilted in a ¾-inch crosshatching. There is some deterioration on the padded areas. Cotton seeds are evident in the batting.

Mary Jane Pierre was born in 1819 in Norfolk, Virginia. William John Robertson was born February 8, 1809, in Norfolk, Virginia. William ran away to sea at the age of nineteen. He and Mary Jane were married in 1833 and made their home in Baltimore, Maryland. They had five children.

Captain Robertson owned a schooner and engaged in shipping and transportation on the Atlantic Coast. He was a member of the American Independent Order of Odd Fellows, I.O.O.F. , Washington Lodge No. 1 of Baltimore. Mary Jane was a member of the Rebekah Lodge, the American founded sister assembly of the Odd Fellows.

In 1849 Captain Robertson sold his schooner and, with ten other men, chartered the vessel *Creole* and sailed around Cape Horn to San Francisco, California. He was not taken with the epidemic of "gold fever," but with San

Captain William John Robertson.

Mary Jane Pierre Robertson.

"The Farm," Whidbey Island, Washington.

Francisco's need for piers and warehouses. He purchased two abandoned vessels and used them for warehousing.

In 1851, after he purchased the brig *Tarquina,* Captain Robertson sent for Mary Jane and the children. He then sailed to the Puget Sound to deliver supplies for the settlers there, and to acquire timber for San Francisco piers. He was so taken with the beautiful Northwest and its possibilities that he searched for and found a land donation claim on the west side of Whidbey Island, Washington Territory, overlooking Admiralty Inlet. There was not only a prairie for farmland, but a forest from which he could cut timber. His claim consisted of two hundred and forty-six acres according to Patent No. 697.

Mary Jane, her children, and her brother Thomas Perry sailed on *Brother Jonathan* to the Isthmus of Panama. It took them twenty-five to thirty days to trek by canoe and mule through the Isthmus of Panama. In Panama City, July 15, 1851, they boarded the steamer *Constitution* and arrived in San Francisco on August 8, 1851.

In 1853 Captain Robertson and his son John returned to Whidbey Island. John remained on the island to live and work the family claim and direct operations, while his father returned to San Francisco for the rest of the family. Their first home, a log cabin, was burned by the Indians. Captain Robertson placed a ship cannon on the property, and from then on, the family remained on the claim without taking refuge at the fort.

In 1859 Captain Robertson was appointed keeper for the new Admiralty Head lighthouse. He served as master of the light for five years. He was also one of the first Puget Sound pilots to take over as captain and bring large ships into the Puget Sound.

Mary Jane died on the homestead on January 8, 1875. Captain Robertson died in Coupeville, Island County, Washington Territory, in 1888. Both are buried in the Sunnyside Cemetery in Coupeville, across from the Whidbey Island blockhouse.

Owned by Jean Lovejoy.

1854
Whig Rose (variation)
73" x 73"

MARY H. CLARK, quiltmaker

Mary H. Clark's Whig Rose quilt is an exquisite work of art. Proud of her delicate work and tiny stitches, Mary worked her initials, M. H. C. in corded relief along the top edge of her quilt. Mary must have been a woman of great patience, for the hours that went into creating the elaborate appliqué and detailed quilting were many.

This unique version of the Whig Rose features 12-inch appliquéd Whig Rose blocks, which alternate with 8-inch muslin squares. Mary trimmed the corners of each appliqué block to accommodate this setting. Inside each 8-inch muslin block is a sprig of grapes, which has been worked in trapunto. The quilting lines, spaced ³⁄₁₆ of an inch apart, accentuate the stuffed work. There is a continuous feather design just inside the appliqué border, which has been quilted. However, only about 10 of these feathers have been stuffed. One wonders if Mary grew ill or just tired of the tedious project and did not finish. Even the appliqué border is an elaborate design of a vine using the bud design from the Whig Rose appliqué blocks with angular leaves.

The quilt was passed on to Mina Marcy Nuttall, who gave the quilt to Mary Nuttall; Mary gave it to the Daughters of the Pioneers of Washington, Walla Walla Chapter 12. They, in turn, donated the quilt to the Fort Walla Walla Museum.

It is ironic that this quilt, fit for a fine mansion, graced a small wooden cabin in Walla Walla. Fort Walla Walla was a lonely outpost in 1854. Barely a year had passed since the territory of Washington had been established, separating it from Oregon. Life was perilous in the settle-

Mary H. Clark.

ment; the memory of the massacre of Marcus and Narcissa Whitman in 1847 lingered in the minds of settlers.

The first Walla Walla compounds or "forts" were built in 1818 by the Northwest Supply Company at the confluence of the Walla Walla and Columbia rivers. In 1825 the Hudson Bay Company constructed a fort at the same sight. But the first official fort to be constructed in Walla Walla was built in 1856 to station the Ninth Infantry. Commanded by Colonel George Wright, their task was to suppress the Indian uprisings among the Yakima, Spokane, and Nez Perce tribes. The Fort Walla Walla Museum complex, built on the site of a permanent military post constructed in 1858, now displays Mary H. Clark's handsome quilt.

Photos and quilt courtesy of the Fort Walla Walla Museum, Walla Walla.

Fort Walla Walla, Washington. (Courtesy of Museum of History and Industry, Seattle)

1855
VARIABLE STAR

97" x 110"

REBECCA MARGARET STALEY HOUCK, quiltmaker

Rebecca Margaret Staley was born May 4, 1820. On May 7, 1855, Rebecca and Frederick Houck were married in Frederick, Frederick County, Maryland. In 1864 Rebecca and Frederick took all of their possessions, including this exquisite and striking Variable Star bride's quilt, by wagon to Tifflin, Seneca County, Ohio. With this move they escaped the Civil War Battle of Monocacy, which took place near Frederick July 4 and 5 of that year. Rebecca's husband was a farmer, yet he enjoyed investing money in stocks and, at one time, ended up losing part of his land. Frederick died in 1891 when a tree fell on him.

Rebecca was accomplished at all kinds of handwork, and though life was hard for her after Frederick's death, she continued to do handwork whenever possible. However, of all the quilts she made, the Variable Star is her masterpiece. There are 143 7½-inch blocks set 11 x 13. Seventy-two of the blocks are hand pieced using indigo blue fabric and set with alternating unpieced white blocks. The 6-inch indigo blue border has a tiny white star design. Was this chosen to go with her pieced Variable Star? The unpieced blocks are quilted with many different quilting designs. Rebecca's stitches are small, even, and straight. She brought the muslin backing to the front to bind the edges, and here her craftsmanship is almost unbelievable. She made a ¹⁄₁₆-inch rolled hem, like the hem on a fine handkerchief, secured with her tiny, tiny stitches. Then, by counting the threads in the cloth, she cross-stitched her name, "Rebecca M. Staley," in red thread at the foot of the quilt.

Rebecca's legacy of handwork was handed down to her great-granddaughter Dorothy Blume. Among the collection is her sampler, completed in 1848, which shows her expertise with the needle and her ability to do a variety of embroidery stitches. Also in the collection is an appliquéd block. Inscribed in ink between two laurel branches on this block is the married name and birth date of Rebecca's daughter Clarissa, "Clarissa E./Baker/1856." Why this block was made and why she chose to use this particular combination—Clarissa's married name and birth date—is uncertain, unless it was meant to be included in a quilt for Clarissa. Both Rebecca and Clarissa were quilters, and it was Clarissa who left this Variable Star quilt to her granddaughter Dorothy Blume.

Owned by Dorothy Blume, Sequim.

Rufus and Clarissa E. Baker.

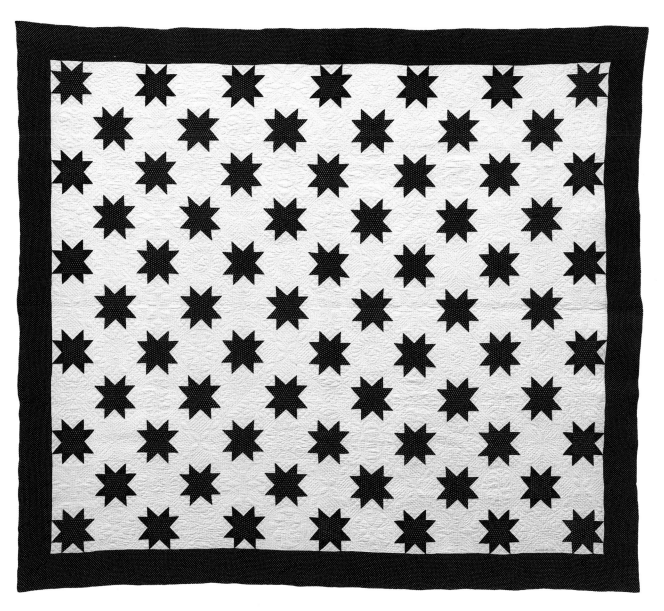

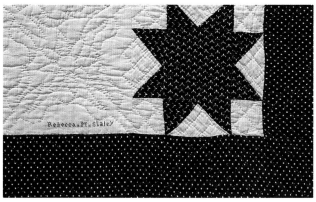

Rebecca M. Staley

c. 1855
BASKET

70″ x 82″

JANE SUMMERS COYLE, quiltmaker

❀ Jane Summers was born August 22, 1841, to Elizabeth and Thomas Summers of Burlington, DesMoines County, Iowa. In 1845 Thomas was made captain of a wagon train heading for the Pacific Northwest. With him were his wife, a son, and two daughters. They left their home in early spring and arrived at the Whitman Mission, Washington Territory, in the late fall of 1845. During the winter of 1845–1846, Jane attended the school that Narcissa Whitman conducted for the Indians and the children of emigrants. Sensing unrest among the Indians and fearing its outcome, Thomas reorganized his train and left for the Willamette Valley in the spring of 1846. On November 27, 1847, the Whitmans and twelve others were massacred. More were taken captive and later released.

The Summers settled near Lebanon, Oregon Territory, where there was a large settlement of emigrants and friendly Indians. They filed for 640 acres in Champoeg County, Oregon Territory. On March 4, 1864, Elizabeth Summers abandoned her husband and children. It was thought that she returned to Ireland, the place of her birth. In order to get clear title to the land, Thomas had to sue Elizabeth for divorce in 1871. Thomas deeded part of the land to Oregon Territory for use as a park (Soda Springs State Park).

Jane married James Bunch Coyle on July 17, 1859, in Sand Ridge, Linn County, Oregon. They lived near Lebanon for nearly seven years. In 1866 they moved to Walla Walla Valley, Walla Walla County, Washington Territory, where they settled on 160 acres, four miles west of Walla Walla on Mill Creek (about three miles from the site of the Whitman Mission). They had ten children.

Originally, their farm produced hay and grain, but later they converted it to one of the county's largest and most modern dairy farms. (The property has since been divided into building lots and is a suburb of the city of Walla Walla.)

On April 29, 1901, James was found dead at his plow. Jane managed to farm for twenty-one years after his death. On April 24, 1922, Jane died on the farm that had been her home for fifty-six years.

If only this Blue Basket quilt could talk! Jane either made this marvelous basket quilt or helped make it, according to family remembrances. The quilt has 42 pieced and appliquéd indigo blue baskets, which are set on point with alternating unpieced blocks. Half of the baskets face one side of the quilt, and the others face the opposite side of the quilt. The quilt has two borders—a 1-inch blue border and a 1½-inch white border. The indigo blue cotton appears to have been hand dyed. All the stitching was done by hand. It was quilted with diagonal lines forming a cross-hatching across the face of the quilt. The backing is of exceptionally fine woven white cotton. Cotton seeds are evident in the cotton batting. The binding was replaced with a commercially made bias binding.

Jane passed the Blue Basket quilt on to her daughter Nida Ann Coyle Timmons. It was later passed on to Jane's grandson Richard Timmons and his wife June Timmons.

Collection of June Timmons, Walla Walla.

KEN NICOLES PHOTOGRAPHY

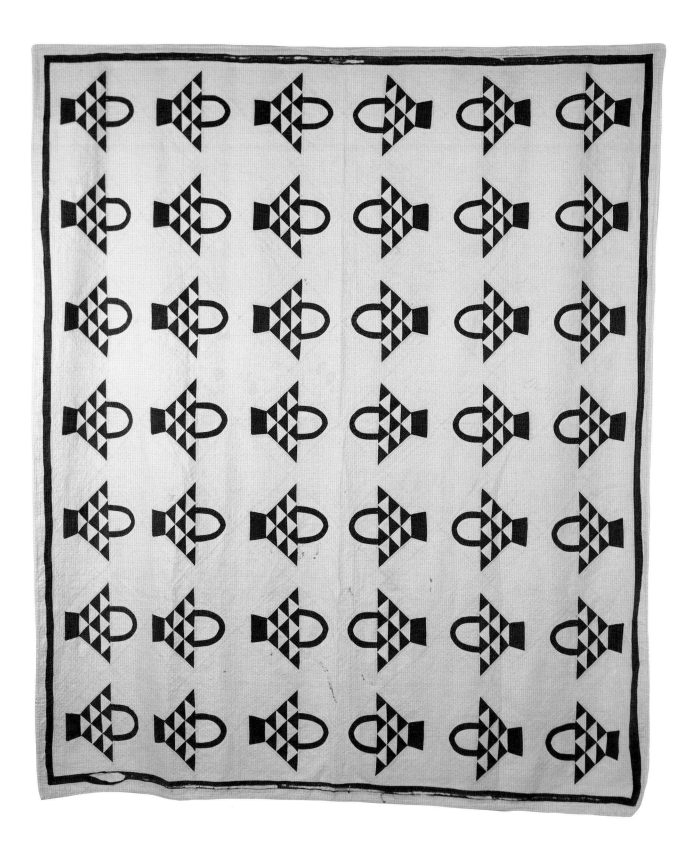

C. 1875
SEVEN SISTERS (variation)

82½" x 85"

EMMA ROBERTS MORGAN, quiltmaker

❧ This stunning red, green, and gold cotton quilt with a white background, made by Emma Roberts prior to her marriage, shows off a color combination that was quite popular in the late 1800s. The quilt is entirely hand pieced and quilted. The stars are pieced with a hexagon center, and elongated triangles form the six points of the stars. Irregular hexagons connect the stars in the center of the piecework, and the resulting 11½-inch circle of stars is pieced into the center of the 14½-inch block. The 7½-inch wide sashing is pieced from solid green, red, and gold cotton fabric. Two opposite sides of this graphic quilt have a 1¼-inch gold cotton border. The edges of the quilt are bound with straight-of-the-grain green cotton binding, which was handmade and has been repaired in several places. The quilt has a lightweight cotton batting; cotton seeds are evident. A strip of gold-colored cotton was added to one side of the white cotton, homespun backing.

Emma quilted straight lines in the sashing using colored thread to match the fabric whenever possible. Her stitches are small and even. The double hearts quilted in the corners of each block (the only hearts in her surviving quilts) indicate that this may have been intended as her wedding quilt.

A similar quilt, which uses the identical block pattern, but a different setting, was located by the Texas Heritage Quilt Society (see the American Quilter's Society's *Texas Quilts, Texas Treasures,* p. 51). Perhaps this pattern was published for the 1876 Centennial of the United States.

Of the many and varied quilts that Emma made, from the 1870s to the early 1940s, only seventeen have survived. These quilts, as well as samplings of her crochet and knit lace on bed linens were handed down to her great-grandson Davi Arthur Petersen.

Emma was born in 1859. She and her parents David and Jane Anderson Roberts came West by way of a wagon in 1870. They settled in Waitsburg, Walla Walla County, Washington Territory, where Emma's father was a minister at the Methodist Episcopal Church.

Young Emma married James W. "J. W." Morgan, age thirty, on October 14, 1877, in Waitsburg. J. W. had come West from Lancaster County, Pennsylvania, in 1872. J. W., who was very active in social and civic affairs, was considered "quite a catch" for a lovely young lady. He operated the pony express between Waitsburg and Spokane. He was the town pharmacist. (His pharmacy was located in the brick building he built on Main Street, where it still stands.) J. W. was also active in the territorial and state legislatures, as well as being the first city treasurer, county commissioner and president of the First National Bank of Waitsburg. With Emma as a gracious hostess and partner to her husband's endeavors—as reported by the local newspapers—it is not surprising that their home was the center of many social and political affairs.

Emma and J. W. were married for fifty years when J. W. died July 13, 1928. After his death, Emma moved to Vancouver, Clark County, Washington, where she died in 1955 at the age of ninety-six. Family members still own the original Walla Walla County homestead.

Owned by Davi Arthur Petersen, Brush Prairie.

Emma Morgan (standing at center) and J. W. Morgan (seated beside her) in front of their home in Waitsburg, Washington.

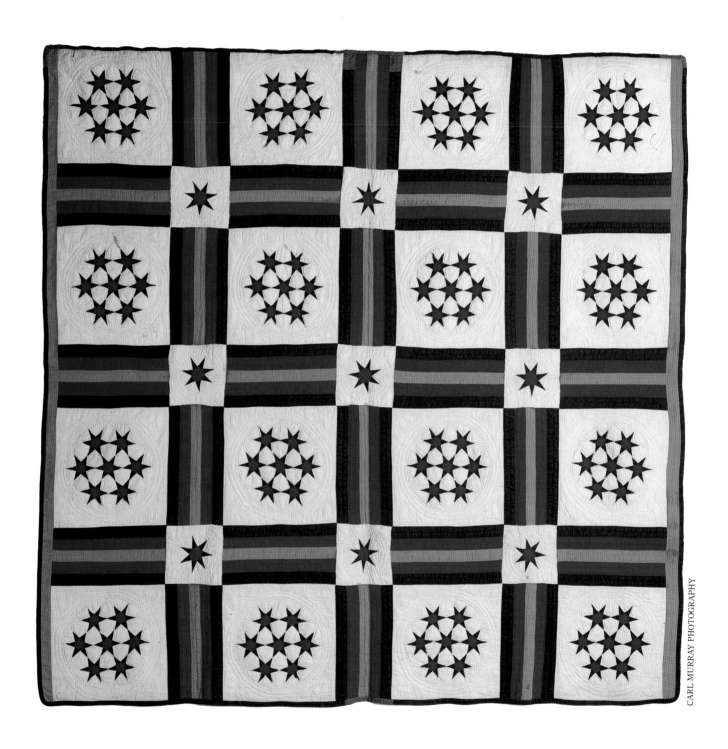

CARL MURRAY PHOTOGRAPHY

c. 1885
CIGAR SILK QUILT

52" x 52"

CLEMENTINE ZILPHA STARLING TECK PEARSON, quiltmaker

Before the 1920s when individual cellophane wrapping was available, a cigar silk (ribbon), bearing the name of the cigar company, was wrapped around the fifty cigars that made up a box of cigars. The silks were ½- to 1½-inches wide and 15- to 18-inches long. Cigar-smoking gentlemen were very fussy about their hand-rolled cigars. They did not want anyone handling them, and the undisturbed silk was a guarantee that no one had tampered with them.

Ladies saved the silks and used them to make many fancy pillows for their husbands or loved ones. Quilts were less common. The Cigar Silk quilt here is made of 16 blocks. All the silks are beautifully feather stitched together. The "fringe" is made from folded short pieces of silks left from the piecing of the blocks. The silks provide an unusual record of the cigar brands available in the area at the turn of the century.

Clementine Zilpha Starling was born January 17, 1860, in Green County, Indiana. She married Irving Teck in 1874. Irving had served in the Civil War and had moved to Washington Territory in 1869. He returned to the East to find a wife. (He lost his first wife and two children to the measles.) Irving worked for the railroad. Clementine and Irving made their way West in a covered wagon, migrant fashion, as Irving worked on the construction of the railroad. It took them seven years to reach Washington Territory. Along the way, they lost their first child to the measles. Clementine helped the Indians take care of their sick.

Clementine and Irving homesteaded on 160 acres in Ellensburg, Kittitas County, Washington Territory. Their daughter Pearl Aimee was born June 4, 1887. Irving died when Pearl was two years old.

Clementine married Sven Pearson in 1890. Sven owned a cigar store, liquor store, and a real estate business in Ellensburg. He saved the silks from the cigar boxes for Clementine. In a fire that destroyed their home, Clementine lost many Indian artifacts that she had collected on her way West.

Clementine's quilt was passed on to her daughter Pearl Aimee, who in turn passed it on to her daughter Dorothy Egan. Dorothy donated the quilt to the Edmonds South Snohomish County Historical Society for their museum in 1979.

Courtesy of the Edmonds South Snohomish County Historical Society, Edmonds

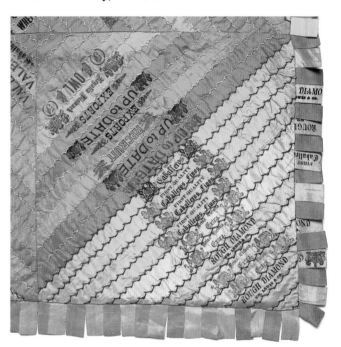

1887
LANCASTER ROSE
72" x 76"

ZILPHA ANN DAVIS AND
ELLEN ALICE DAVIS, quiltmakers

Zilpha Ann was born November 3, 1834. She married Woodford J. Davis April 2, 1857. Their daughter Ellen Alice was born November 12, 1859 in Vincennes, Knox County, Indiana. When Ellen Alice met and fell in love with John Depew, she and her mother began this quilt so that Ellen Alice would have a quilt to take to her new home. Ellen Alice and John Depew were married in 1887. Their daughter Susanne was born in 1891. In 1895 the Depew family traveled by wagon to Idaho. Not much later, they moved to a homestead on Toad Lake Hill, Bellingham, Whatcom County, Washington. Susanne Depew was married in Bellingham in 1916.

This quilt was not used, but rather stored in a trunk at the foot of the bed and only brought out for airing and to be admired several times each year. When Susanne died, her daughter Mavis Taylor inherited the trunk and the quilt, as she was the family member who loved handwork.

Mavis reminisces that her grandmother Ellen Alice worked exceptionally hard and that her grandfather John Depew was not terribly ambitious. He walked eight to nine miles a day just to go fishing, and sat on an apple box instead of standing to hoe the corn. Zilpha Ann died in 1898. Ellen Alice died in 1924.

Mavis is the fourth generation of women in this family who have quilted. She quilts in a frame using her great-grandmother's and grandmother's quilt frame clamps.

This Lancaster Rose is so charming you want to reach out to embrace it. There are four 24-inch blocks that form the center part of the quilt. The appliqué is made with red,

Ellen Alice Depew (right) on her homestead with unidentified neighbor.

yellow-orange, and two shades of green cotton, as well as a light pink printed cotton all on a white background. There is outline quilting around the appliqués, hearts quilted in among the flowers, and feathers quilted next to the appliquéd roses. The borders are quilted with cross-hatching. Three sides have 12-inch borders, and the fourth side has an 8-inch border. Only two of the 12-inch borders have an appliquéd vine, leaves, and flower design. Another two-bordered quilt can be found in *American Patchwork Quilts* by Lenice Ingram Bacon (plate 31). "... This quilt has its practical side. Evidently, it was made for a bed that would stand in the corner of the room, perhaps the living room. Since on the back and far side none of the border motif would show, it was done to be seen and admired only on one side and across the foot of the bed. Bacon Collection." It is also possible that the ladies ran out of fabric or time before the wedding. Regardless of the reason, it is a most appealing quilt.

Owned by Mavis Taylor, Lynden.

Ellen Alice Depew's quilt frame clamps.

c. 1890
LOG CABIN—BARN RAISING
70" x 79"

ELLA MATTESON SMITH, quiltmaker

Ella Matteson was born in Lafayette, Pennsylvania, February 5, 1857. This slender, black-haired woman married her cousin, Sheldon Smith June 15, 1886. They traveled West to Washington Territory that same year. Sheldon brought Ella to a homestead in Mannette, near Bremerton, Kitsap County, overlooking the waters of Puget Sound. He built their log cabin on a hill away from the tides, as Ella was afraid of the Indian women who gathered clams along the shore and who peered at her curiously.

They had three children, two of whom survived and grew up on the homestead: Olive, born July 27, 1888, and David, born February 11, 1892. Sheldon contributed land to build a school, where Olive went through the eighth grade. When Olive grew up, she was active in music and art societies in Seattle. She was one of the first women to attend Stanford University, which she paid for by selling land in Bremerton that she had inherited.

In 1913 Ella made her only journey "back East" to visit her family. While she was gone, Sheldon built her a new home—without a single closet or cupboard. Ella complained about this omission as long as she lived in the house. Ella sewed all the family clothing, did exquisite raised white-on-white work, which took prizes at the county fairs, and darned socks or pieced every evening. She kept her basket of scraps by the wood stove. In the winter she would piece for hours by lantern light and when spring came, she would order cotton batting to

Three Matteson sisters; Ella Matteson (center).

finish the quilt. Ella died March 11, 1938.

This all-silk log cabin, set in the barn-raising design, was never used as a bed covering. The top is entirely hand stitched; the cotton backing was added by machine. This graphic quilt has a crazy-patch border. The predominance of black fabric is due to the mode of dress in the late nineteenth century. The quilt had been stored in a family trunk for at least thirty-five years, until it was recently hung in Ella's great-granddaughter Barbara Lockwood Johnston's law office.

Owned by Barbara Lockwood Johnston, Woodinville.

Log house, Manette, Washington.

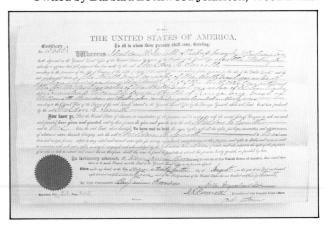

Smith family land grant, 1891, Kitsap County, Washington Territory.

1898
DUTCHMAN'S PUZZLE

75″x 88″

TECLA COFFEE RIPPETEAU, quiltmaker

Tecla Coffee was born in 1833 in Kentucky. She married John Rippeto in 1853. John was born in 1829. John's grandfather William Rippeto, Sr. served in the Revolutionary War "... and assisted in establishing American Independence, while acting in the capacity of a private in the 14th Virginia Regiment ..." (from a War Department letter dated 1928 and addressed to J. J. Rippeteau, St. John, Washington).

John and Tecla Coffee Rippeteau lived most of their lives in Kansas. They had nine children. At the urging of one of their children, they changed the spelling of their surname from Rippeto back to the French, Rippeteau. The Rippeteau family is said to have fled France in the late 1600s to avoid religious persecution.

Tecla made this quilt shortly after the birth of her granddaughter Corrinne Cadwallader Rippeteau Howard in 1895. Tecla died only seven years later in 1902. Corrinne's family moved from Portland, Oregon, her birthplace, to Washington State, where she remained for the rest of her life. She died in Colfax, Whitman County, Washington in 1986. The quilt and an attached note stating who and when it was made were given to Corrinne's granddaughter Sally J. Howard.

Tecla's Dutchman's Puzzle quilt was made with twenty-eight 10-inch blocks and four half blocks. The sashing is a purple and black print. It is unusual to see this much purple fabric on a quilt from this period, because stable, nonbleeding purple fabric was difficult to obtain. This piece of work is a fine example of Tecla's creativity. It is also an example of how, with this particular pattern and the use of scraps, color placement can change the appearance of a block. These blocks are all the same pattern, but the color placement has made some pieced blocks look like swastikas and others like windmills; one red and black block looks like a spinning pinwheel. After the blocks were set, Tecla quilted parallel lines across the center and diagonal lines on the border.

Owned by Sally J. Howard, Seattle.

Corrine Howard, six years.

c. 1900
LONE STAR

63" x 76"

MARY EVAZE CLARK COCHRAN CLARK, quiltmaker

Mary Evaze Clark was born December 16, 1861, in Missouri. Mary married a Mr. Cochran and had one child. After Cochran died, Mary married her cousin William Pleasant Clark. They had five children. The family moved to Eastern Washington in the 1920s. In 1921 they settle in Mabton, Yakima County, Washington. Mary was an accomplished seamstress as well as a quilter. She was active and kept her own house and garden until 1958, when she died in a fire that destroyed her home in Mabton.

Mary made this hand-pieced and hand-quilted graphic quilt when she lived in Missouri. She even used some of her husband's baby clothes in the piecing. The drafting of the Lone Star, with pieced border and corner blocks, is a tribute to her mathematical knowledge. The half-block triangles at the side centers are the same pattern as the corners, but they have been redrafted to accommodate the large scale required. The 2-inch border is broken by the tips of the Lone Star. The top and the bottom of the quilt has a 4-inch pieced border, which echoes the pieced flower bud from the corner blocks. Several fabrics bind the edge of the quilt. The fabric is cut on the straight of the grain. The stitching is by hand. Outline quilting and quilted parallel lines enhance this masterpiece.

Mary gave the Lone Star to her great-grandson Lee Charles Clark. Lee loved to visit his great-grandmother and get special crackers for a treat.

Owned by Lee Charles Clark, Yakima.

C. 1900
FEATHERED WORLD WITHOUT END

60″ x 72″

THERESA M. STODDARD FANCHER, quiltmaker

This handsome Feathered World Without End quilt reflects an ambitious piecer. Not only are there forty-two 10-inch blocks, but each block has 85 pieces. The blocks are set 6 x 7. After Theresa finished her hand piecing and set the top together, she hand quilted it with a feathered design in the 26 white triangular areas around the edges of the quilt and in the 72 white, diamond-shaped areas created by the indigo blue and white pieced pattern. The quilting makes the back of the quilt as attractive as the front. The quilt is bound with a ¼-inch matching indigo blue binding. It is a wonderful example of the beauty that can be created by the needle.

The phrase "world without end" can be found in several places in the Bible and is common to many Christian prayers: "Glory be to the Father, and to the Son, and to the Holy Ghost, as it was in the Beginning, is now and ever shall be, world without end. Amen." Shakespeare, Kipling, and other writers and poets used the term. *The Dictionary of American Idioms* defines "world without end" as a literary phrase meaning: endlessly, forever, eternally. Each human being has to die, but there is hope that mankind will go on world without end. (Or that life will go on forever.) This certainly describes this pattern, which appears to be spinning, never ending.

Theresa M. Stoddard was born October 13, 1861, in Mahaska County, Iowa. She married Joseph M. Fancher. She came to Washington State on an immigrant train and ranched in Yakima Valley. Theresa and Joseph had three children: William Dennis born December 27, 1889, in Boone County, Iowa; Grace born July 15, 1891, in Woodward, Iowa; and Helen Louisa born April 6, 1894, in Iowa. The quilt was passed on to Grace who married Warren Reynolds, an apple grower in Yakima Valley. They had a son, Joseph Dixon Reynolds. When Grace died January 6, 1979, the quilt was given to Warren's cousin Harry Collett. The Collett family moved to the lower valley of Yakima County, Washington, between 1915 and 1917. Harry passed the quilt on to his daughter Beverly J. Ogburn.

Collection of Beverly J. Ogburn, Wapato.

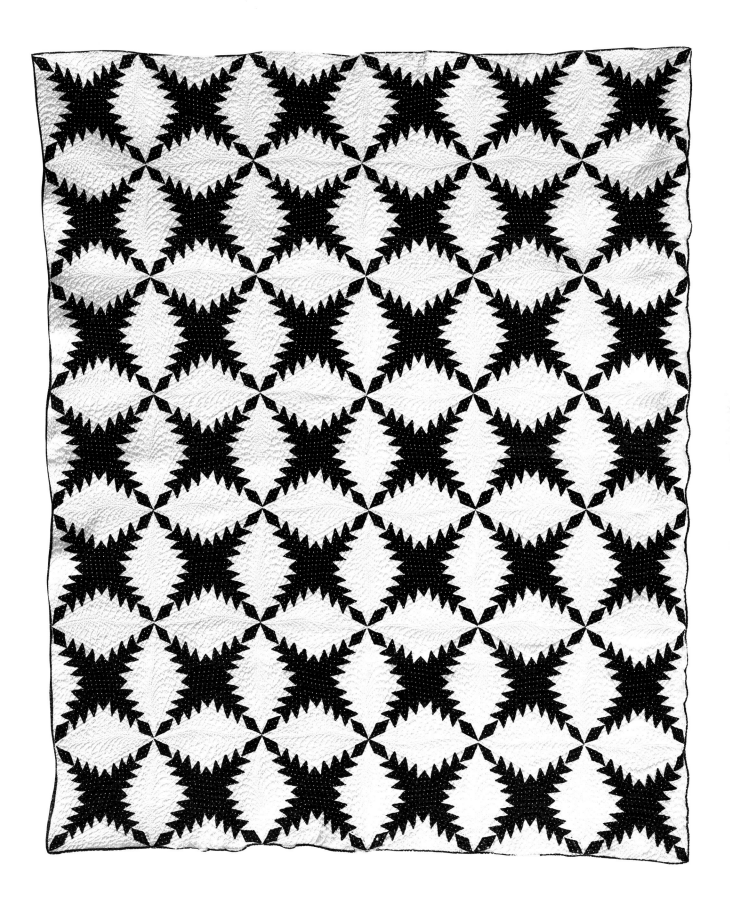

c. 1900
RAILROAD AND DEPOT

61″ x 84″

VIOLA JOHNSON WEST, quiltmaker

Viola Johnson was born June 16, 1878, to John A. and Katherine Stoltz Johnson at Howard Lake, Minnesota. She was one of six children. Viola came to Washington Territory when she was nine years old. In 1901 she married Lausen West. They had no children. They farmed north of Davenport, Lincoln County, Washington, until retirement, when they moved to Cheney, Spokane County, Washington.

According to stories, Lausen West, when nearing middle age, ran off with a young girl. It is said that Viola sent the sheriff after him. He returned to Viola after his escapade, but their relations remained strained from then on.

Viola was an artist as well as a quilter. She did a number of paintings that are treasured by her relatives. Viola's sister Lucretia Johnson Weygant taught art at Eastern Washington State College in Cheney, Washington. Paintings by the two sisters were exhibited in art shows at Cheney. Some of their paintings are in the permanent collection of the Eastern Washington State University.

Viola died April 19, 1965, at age 86 in Cheney. She is buried in Spokane. She left this quilt to her niece, Myrtle Lowary, who donated it to the Lincoln County Historical Society.

Railroad and Depot is also known as Wild Goose Chase-Stars. The twelve 19-inch blocks are set on the straight with a 2½-inch pieced border on all four sides. The backing is brought to the front and machine stitched in place (the only machine stitching on the quilt). The corners are slightly rounded. The quilting is diagonal lines radiating out from each star ½-inch apart. Each large white triangle is quilted with four teardrop shapes. There is some fabric fading and deterioration.

Collection of the Lincoln County Historical Society, Davenport.

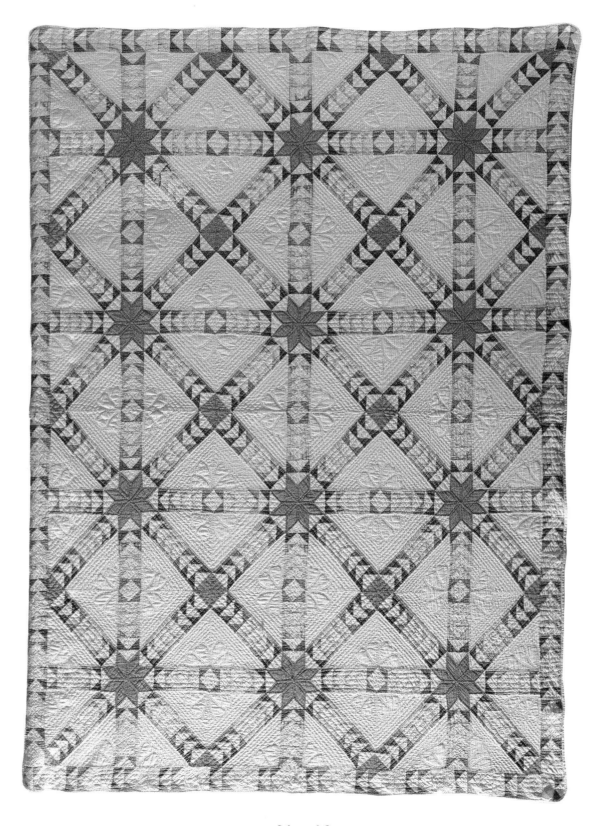

c. 1900
CROWN OF THORNS
73" x 87"

ELLEN VESPER GORDON, quiltmaker

Ellen Vesper Gordon.

Ellen Vesper was born in Thetford, Orange County, Vermont, May 27, 1850. As a girl she moved by covered wagon to Wisconsin, where, at age sixteen, she married William Gordon on February 23, 1866. William served in the Union Army.

Their first son was born in 1867. They had six children in all: five boys and one girl. In 1885 when their oldest son was eighteen, the family moved to a homestead in Deuel County, South Dakota. There they built the first frame house in Deuel County from lumber that was shipped by train. All their livestock came by train, too.

Ellen missed the dandelions that grew in Wisconsin, so her mother sent her some roots to plant. Ellen sewed and knitted for her family. When the children were grown and moved to their own homes, she made quilt tops for each of her five son's families. Ellen died December 8, 1933.

In 1964 Ellen's granddaughter Leona Gordon Harleman took the Crown of Thorns top to the Valley Christian Church in Wapato, Washington, where she served as a parish worker. There she taught women who were living at the Yakima Indian Mission how to quilt. The women did not like Leona's first choice of backing, so she purchased more. Leona stitched the commercially made binding on by hand. The quilting is uneven with knots, but a true piece of American folk art.

The Crown of Thorns pattern is known by other names: Mill Wheel, Wedding Ring, and Rolling Stone.

Owned by Leona Gordon Harleman, Yakima.

Indian women quilting, Valley Christian Church, Wapato, Washington.

c. 1900
FEATHERED STAR

84" x 91"

MARGARET COCHRAN MCCROSKEY, quiltmaker

This handsome, graphic Feathered Star quilt is in excellent condition. The exceptional workmanship makes it a visual treat. It is hand pieced, and the pieced blocks are set on point with alternating unpieced blocks. Margaret planned her sawtooth zigzag border so that it turns the corner without interrupting the design. The edge of this marvelous quilt is hand bound with home-cut matching cotton bias binding. The corners are rounded. Margaret Cochran McCroskey quilted cross-hatching and feathers with quilting stitches (18 to the inch) that are close, straight, and even.

Margaret was born July 3, 1863, in Monroe County, Tennessee. She moved to Washington Territory in 1886 with her sister and brother-in-law, the P. W. Ketrells. They settled on the Camas Prairie, Klickitat County, Washing-ton Territory. Margaret married Samuel M. McCroskey at the home of her brother, J. E. Cochran, five miles east of Colfax, Whitman County, Washington Territory, December 1, 1886. Samuel was born December 28, 1859, in Monroe County, Tennessee. He came West in 1883. During his lifetime, Samuel was an educator, county auditor, and city clerk (for Colfax). Margaret and Samuel renewed their wedding vows on their fiftieth wedding anniversary in 1936. Margaret died in Colfax in 1953.

Margaret was an excellent quilter and made many quilts. Her granddaughter Joan Dorr said, "Grandma was probably one of the truly good people in the world. She was never cross, never unkind, always loving and patient. She was very dear."

Collection of Darlene Broughton, Dayton.

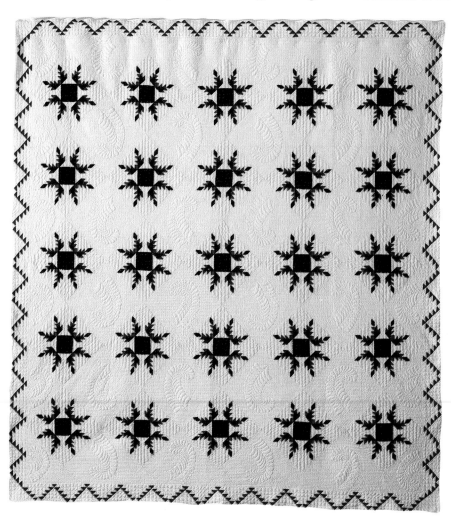

1910
FEATHERED STAR

74" x 92"

MARION SHIELLS PERKINS, quiltmaker

Marion Shiells was born May 15, 1881, in Wittonstall, Northumberland, England. She was the daughter of John Shiells and Emmeline Hankey. Marion immigrated with her parents to the United States in 1882. Marion married George L. Perkins August 27, 1902, in Galt, Kansas. They had seven daughters. Marion died in 1972 in Twin Falls, Twin Falls County, Idaho.

Marion pieced the Feathered Star top between 1909 and 1910, when she was expecting her daughter Frances. The top was hand quilted in 1937 by Marion's daughter Ruth Perkins Compton and Ruth's husband Ray. When the quilting was completed, the quilt was given to Frances Perkins (Bennett).

The gray and white fabrics are from old dresses worn by Marion's mother Emmeline while she was still in England. The 20 pieced blocks are set together with 4½-inch printed pink cotton sashing. The batting is a medium-weight cotton. The edge is bound with a home-cut, straight-of-the-grain binding.

Owned by Frances Perkins Bennett, Prosser.

Marion Shiells Perkins.

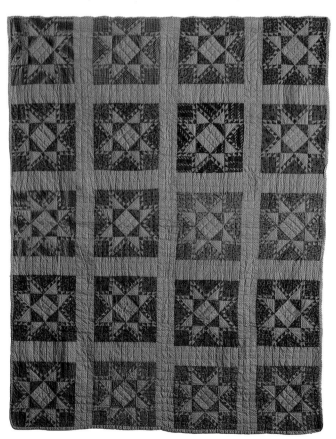

1905
CRAZY QUILT

63½″ x 73″

MINNIE HARWOOD BELL WOOD, quiltmaker

Minnie Harwood Bell Wood and Harry E. Wood.

This outstanding quilt is practically all silk; there are none of the velvets and other heavy fabrics that are found in many crazy quilts. Minnie Harwood Bell took special care to use all like-weight fabrics. She also used a wide variety of exceptionally well-executed, decorative embroidery stitches on the thirty 12-inch blocks and the one 5-inch border. In addition to the decorative stitches joining patches, she embroidered the bust of a girl in a bonnet, three stems of cherries, a blue bird on a branch, a blue vase, an anchor, and an owl holding a parasol with "Owl Maid" embroidered under the branch. There are also two owls on a branch, one wearing a bonnet, the other a hat with "We're from the owl'd county" stitched underneath (see McMorris, P. *Crazy Quilts,* p. 55), appliquéd butterflies and pansies, embroidered initials, and painted patches.

The important historical features of this quilt are the souvenir- and campaign-imprinted ribbons that Minnie saved and added to her crazy patching. Some of the ribbons included are: a pink "VOTE FOR OLYMPIA FOR THE CAPITAL"; a red "SEATTLE TACOMA W. W. I. E. Sept, 26, 1891" (Western Washington Industrial Exposition); a blue on white "WELCOME Wednesday May 6, 1891, Seattle, Wash., Benjamin Harrison, Twenty-Third President of the United States;" ... a red "LINCOLN REPUBLICAN CLUB OF OLYMPIA"; a red railroad ribbon imprinted "THE GREAT NORTHERN, Nov. 27–28, 1891, We rejoice in the completion of the Washington and British Columbia section." Another ribbon "1636 Harvard University 1886" may have been saved by a family member and given to Minnie for her quilt. There are other ribbons, labels, and wonderful cloth patches with faces of children and young girls. There are two ribbons in lovely soft colors with Kate Greenaway children. One 3½-inch-wide ribbon has young girls sitting on a fence (see McMorris, P. *Crazy Quilts,* p. 76). The other 3-inch-wide ribbon has young girls walking from left to right.

Minnie was born May 13, 1869 in Wellfleet, Norfolk County, Massachusetts. In 1891 she traveled West with her mother and stepfather to homestead near Sunnydale, King County, Washington, south of Seattle. It was here that she became a schoolteacher of all twelve grades in a one-room schoolhouse. Minnie married Henry E. Wood September 25, 1894. Henry's family had been homesteading in the Seattle area since 1877. As a young man he learned to converse with the local Indians using Chinook jargon. In 1900 Henry was a postal carrier for the old Arlington Post Office in Seattle; later he worked out of the Georgetown branch. The house Henry built for Minnie still stands.

Minnie made many quilts and sewed clothing for her family and, in particular, her two granddaughters. The girls loved to find scraps from their clothing in their grandmother's quilts. Minnie died March 23, 1953 in her Seattle home. Her granddaughter Eleanor Jeanne Prata Carlson inherited this Crazy Quilt and her size 8 sterling silver thimble. There are holes worn through the apex of the thimble from so much use.

Owned by Eleanor Jeanne Prata Carlson, Seattle.

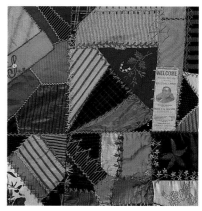

1915
SWASTIKA DOLL QUILT

20" x 24"

LIZZIE ANN HENDERSON SKEIE, quiltmaker

Lizzie Ann Henderson was born January 2, 1874. She married February 1, 1893. Lizzie, her husband Sven Skeie, and seven children lived on a farm near Randall, Hamilton County, Iowa. She made this marvelous red-and-white doll quilt with loving stitches for her daughter Beulah Skeie. Lizzie pieced this quilt with solid red cotton and off-white muslin. The backing is muslin, and the muslin binding is handmade on the straight of the grain. Her hand quilting is delightful. She made many quilts and hand dyed some of her brown cottons with walnuts.

Lizzie raised chickens and mailed them to customers. She also showed them at fairs, against the wishes of both her husband and her father. Her engraved business card bore her name and an illustration of her chickens. She was a determined business woman. Lizzie died February 15, 1962.

Beulah treasured her doll quilt and took good care of it. Beulah passed her dolls, this doll quilt, and a doll rocking chair (handmade by her father) on to her own daughter Marilyn "Mickey" Runkel. Mickey remembers receiving this special quilt and the dolls and how she loved to play with them. She also remembers that, in the 1930s, the swastika became the symbol of the National Socialist party in Germany, and how from then on, people associated the swastika with Hitler's Germany and World War II. Mickey started turning the quilt back-side-out when wrapping up her doll so her friends would not see the swastikas, just the lovely quilting. It was sad for her to have to hide what was made and given in love. But she continued to care for her doll quilt, and she still treasures it today, as is evident by the quilt's excellent condition after being well used.

Three generations of women have played with this quilt, doll, and rocker. They reside in a corner of the Hemstad library, where they are still played with on special occasions.

The swastika symbol was used in ancient cultures all over the world. It had a variety of meanings; it was a sign of good luck and good will, as well as a symbol of the Greek cross in the Christian Church. For American Indians, the swastika represented the four winds, rivers, mountains, and rains.

Lizzie would be proud of her granddaughter Mickey Runkel Hemstad, who is a painter and fiber artist. Mickey has four 18-foot-long tapestries hanging in Schmidt Hall at the University of Washington, and many of her paintings are in private collections. Mickey's husband was an aide to Governor Dan Evans and a state senator from 1980 to 1984.

Collection of Marilyn "Mickey" Runkel Hemstad, Olympia.

Lizzie Ann Henderson Skeie and her chickens.

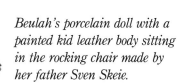
STEVE VENTO PHOTOGRAPHY

Beulah's porcelain doll with a painted kid leather body sitting in the rocking chair made by her father Sven Skeie.

1919
CARPENTER'S SQUARE

64″ x 78½″

EMMA SCHUPPNER CHEESMAN AND
SOPHIA SCHUPPNER FISHER, quiltmakers

Emma Schuppner and her twin brother were born May 18, 1874, in Wisconsin on their twenty-year-old sister Sophia's wedding day; she was marrying Frederick Fisher. Sophia, who was born in Philadelphia, Pennsylvania, was the oldest in this family of ten children; Emma was the youngest. The two of them were the only girls in the family. Emma married a Presbyterian minister, Joseph Franklin Cheesman. They homesteaded in White Earth, Williams County, North Dakota. In April of 1919 Emma and her husband and children moved to Spokane, Spokane County, Washington. Sophia, by then a widow, moved with them and lived with the family. The sisters were quite close, despite their age difference, and did many things together. They made this graphic Carpenter's Square quilt shortly after moving to Washington State in 1919.

This unusual quilt, whose pattern is difficult and rarely used, is made entirely of two cottons: a good-quality, white cotton broadcloth and an indigo blue cotton print. The print is white five-pointed stars on a indigo blue background. Apparently, the fabric was purchased at two different times or from two different bolts, because while the print is identical, one fabric has faded more than the other. The two identical prints are intermingled throughout the quilt top, so the faded indigo is noticeable when looking at the pieced Carpenter's Square blocks. Emma and Sophia did accurate machine piecing. They hand quilted it with small, even, and straight stitches. They quilted a feathered design in the white cross-shaped areas, ¾-inch cross-hatching in the white squares, and ¾-inch diagonal lines on the balance of the quilt.

Emma passed the quilt on to her daughter Esther Cheesman Miller, who in turn passed it on to her son Ken Miller and his wife Joyce. The quilt, it turns out, had been used as a mattress pad for some time, and when the Millers inherited it, three of the edges had been folded in twice onto the quilt top and then machine stitched in place to form a new binding, which spoiled the design of the quilt. The fourth side had a wide piece of sheeting stitched over the edge onto the front (perhaps a moustache guard; all the Cheesman men had mustaches). Joyce carefully restored the quilt by washing out the stains and removing all of the machine stitching around the four edges to return the quilt to its original size. The original, hand-

Sophia Schuppner Fisher.

*Emma Schuppner Cheesman and
Joseph Franklin Cheesman.*

made, white cotton binding was still intact, though a bit worn. The binding was cut on the straight of the grain and machine stitched in place.

Collection of Ken and Joyce Miller, Edmonds.

c. 1920
OCEAN WAVES

70" x 76"

JANET DOVE MAYBEE MARTIN, quiltmaker

❧ Janet Dove was six months old when her parents and four brothers and sisters joined an 1877 wagon train in Kansas for the long, tedious journey West. The family settled in the little village of Weston, Umatilla County, Oregon, at the foot of the Blue Mountains. A family of seven required a lot of bedding and Janet's mother Mary Jane always had a basket of quilt pieces handy to work on. Little Janet was fascinated with these blocks, and at a very early age, she learned to sew together simple blocks. Her love of quilting lasted all of her life.

Janet attended school in a little schoolhouse, which her father built on a corner of his homestead. (This building still stands.) On May 10, 1896, Janet married George Martin, a young man from Missouri. They had four children. In 1908 they moved to the booming town of Mabton, Yakima County, Washington. There they opened a general mercantile store and sold everything from groceries, dry goods, and hardware to coal, oil, and shoes. Each year salesmen brought a huge, new sample book of wool swatches for men's mail-order suits. Janet then made the old samples into quilts. She made log cabin quilts, quilts of just the square samples sewn together, and crazy quilts, which she embellished with variations of the feather stitch. The store sold other fabrics, and Janet used the cotton remnants and scraps from her three girls' dresses to make quilts.

Quilting bees were an important social function in Janet's life. When a quilt was ready to go on the quilting frame, she would set it up in the parlor and invite her friends to help quilt. These early quilts were utilitarian. Janet sent each of her children to college with a special quilt for their dormitory bed. When Janet became a grandmother, she made a quilt for each of the grandchildren. Not realizing the value of these early quilts, the family used them until they wore out, left them behind in moving, or cast them aside in favor of more modern bedding.

This Ocean Waves quilt is hand pieced and hand quilted. Janet showed her artistic abilities in the arrangement of colors. One block appears to be a multicolored scrap block, while all the rest are made either of various indigo blues and white or various red and white cottons.

In the 1930s Janet started making quilts for the beauty of the quilt, not for family bedding. Sometimes she bought new fabric. The patterns she used included: the Double Wedding Ring, Sunbonnet Babies, Butterflies,

Janet Dove Maybee Martin and George Martin.

and Grandmother's Flower Garden among others. Some quilts are signed with her name, the date, and the recipient of the quilt. Today, her family cherishes all these quilts; some have been handed down, mother to daughter, granddaughter to great-granddaughter. Janet's great-granddaughter Elizabeth Erickson Sevy has been greatly influenced by the beauty of Janet's quilts. She designs and makes beautiful quilts of her own. Janet died April 19, 1957, in Poulsbo, Kitsap County, Washington, leaving a wonderful legacy of beautiful quilts.

Owned by Esther Eileen Martin Ness, Poulsbo.

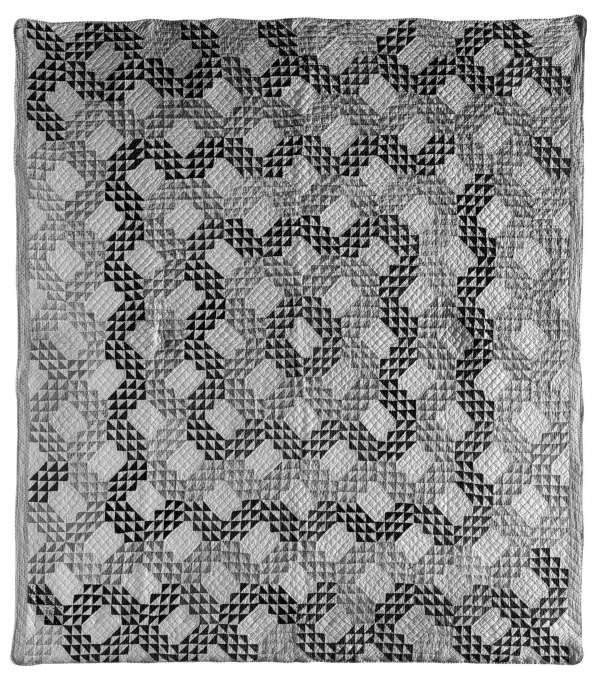

1924
MAPLE LEAF
74" x 74"
ELIZA JANE KEYSER ROWLEY, quiltmaker

Eliza Jane Keyser was born in 1868. She married Charles Rowley in 1894 in Keysers Corner, Canada. In 1906 the Rowleys moved to Gig Harbor, Pierce County, Washington. They had six children, the last of which was born in Gig Harbor. Charles worked as a logger, and quite appropriately, the Rowleys lived on a houseboat on Puget Sound. One day, while moving the houseboat to a new location, the float log was dislodged. The floor split, and all the family possessions in that end of the houseboat went to the bottom of Puget Sound, including a large trunk of family keepsakes and the family Bible.

Eventually the family homesteaded in Wheeler County in eastern Oregon. They raised sheep and carded the wool. With the wool Eliza Jane knit socks, mittens, scarves, and sweaters for the family. Reluctant to let anything go to waste, she dyed the worn-out family underwear and made it into hooked rugs. She also made over her sister-in-law's hand-me-down clothes for her five girls. Two of the girls remember that the clothes were mostly browns, and some were dark plaids.

In 1918 the Rowleys moved once again. Their parade over the Santiam Pass consisted of two wagons loaded with the eight-member family, family goods, cats, a dog, and rabbits followed by a trail of cows and eight horses. It took two weeks to make the trip, camping along the way, cooking over a campfire, and sleeping out. At her new home in Foster, Linn County, Oregon, Eliza Jane had a large vegetable garden; she was especially fond of her flowers and houseplants. Charles often remarked that she thought more of her plants than she did of him. There was no lawn in the yard, just flowers.

In the early 1930s, after her last daughter left home, Eliza Jane helped organize the Jolly Stitchers, a quilting club. At first they met in each other's homes. Later, they bought a small building and had it moved to the grade school. The school used the building every day except the one day a week that the Jolly Stitchers met. Fifty years later, this building is still the meeting place of the Jolly Stitchers and the local kindergarten. All of Eliza Jane's daughters quilted, and two of them are still members of the quilting club.

Eliza Jane made this Maple Leaf quilt in 1924 for the marriage of her daughter Eava Rowley Schmid. There are 36 machine-pieced 12-inch blocks made from dress and shirt scraps. The leaf stem is topstitched to the cor-

Eliza Jane Keyser Rowley and children.

ner patch of the block. The Shaker gray back is brought to the front to bind the edge of the quilt. The hand quilting is in the Baptist Fan (Rainbow) pattern. The quilt has been used very little. It is treasured by Eliza Jane's great-granddaughter Patricia Schmid Gray, also a quilter. Eliza Jane died November 25, 1952.

Collection of Patricia Schmid Gray, Woodinville.

c. 1925
Scrap Medallion

68″ x 84″

Ella Janette Brown Robertson Vickery, quiltmaker

Ella Janette Brown, affectionately called "Nette," was born in 1858 in Iowa. Her family moved to Kansas to farm in 1876. She married Quincy Robertson. They had two children, one of whom died in infancy. While in Kansas the family was victim of an Indian raid. The Indians killed nineteen of the Robertson's large, fat cattle. The loss was a hard financial blow to the family, which made its living raising cattle.

In 1879 the three-generation family moved to Palouse City, Whitman County, Washington Territory, with six wagons of possessions. A few years later, the family moved again, this time to an area in Snoqualmie Valley, Washington Territory, which in 1887 became Fall City, King County, Washington Territory. They purchased twenty-seven acres of railroad land at $2.50 per acre, built a home of cedar boards, and farmed. The first thing that "PaPa" did each time they relocated was purchase a cow. Every fall Ella Janette would pick hops. In 1889 Ella Janette lost her husband and daughter Celia to diptheria.

After the loss of her first husband, Ella Janette moved to Seattle. She worked as a seamstress until her marriage to Mr. Vickery at the New England Hotel in Seattle. They returned to Fall City to live. In 1893 Ella Janette gave birth to a daughter while in Chicago for the Columbian Exposition. Her second husband died in 1917.

This wonderful hand-pieced medallion quilt has over six thousand multicolored pieces of printed, solid-colored, and calico cottons. Ella Janette commented that "99 percent of this quilt is used fabric." She was a very frugal lady, who saved everything her whole life, and was

Ella J. Brown Vickery, ninetieth birthday.

always working on a quilt "one was always in the frame."

The miniature blocks range in size from 1⅞ inches to 3 inches and are set with 1½-inch-wide red, yellow-orange, and green solid cottons. The center of the medallion contains eight 8-pointed pieced stars. The miniature blocks are smaller than many of the blocks pieced today for the popular miniature quilts. There are several mini sizes of pieced "Pinwheel" and the "Double X" block. This is a wonderful example of cottons made during the late nineteenth and early twentieth centuries. Scraps must have been saved for years, or blocks for this quilt were in progress over a long span of time.

Ella Janette gave this quilt to her grandson Austin when he married. Austin and Betty Jo Wiggins used it as a bedspread until they replaced it with a store-bought one some years later. Ella Janette died in Issaquah, King County, Washington, in 1949.

Owned by Mr. and Mrs. Austin Wiggins, Issaquah.

Ella Janette (right) and family.

c. 1930
CRANES

82" x 98"

HANNAH HAYNES HEADLEE, quiltmaker

Hannah Headlee (right) with her brother Clif and niece Pauline.

❀ This remarkable quilt is the original work of quilt artist Hannah Haynes Headlee of Topeka, Shawnee County, Kansas. Hannah was born in Topeka in 1866. She was considered "the artist in the family," and when times were hard, she earned a little money by teaching china painting and watercolor in her home, and by accepting orders for hand-painted china. By 1910 she was married for the third and last time to Jay Headlee. Members of her family looked down on her for her multiple marriages, which were uncommon at that time. In fact, when Hannah's niece Pauline Haynes wanted to take watercolor lessons from Hannah, it was allowed only with the provision that the lessons take place on the front porch. The inside of Hannah's house was strictly off-limits.

In 1914 Pauline was accepted to the New York School of Fine and Applied Art. Hannah accompanied Pauline to New York as a chaperon, and Hannah earned their room and board by painting china. This was the beginning of a close bond that developed between the two.

In the early 1930s Hannah pieced a Grandmother's Flower Garden, her first quilt, and her last pieced quilt. Her artistic abilities showed through even in this first quilt; the color coordination is stunning. Her next two quilts are called Blue Geometrics, and even though they are a geometric design, they are appliquéd.

It is evident from a couple of quilts that Pauline had some influence on Hannah's designs. Pauline went through a "peacock" period, and Hannah made a magnificent appliquéd Peacock quilt. Hannah's Cranes quilt carries some of the same art nouveau characteristics apparent in her Peacock quilt and echoes some of the details of Pauline's paintings.

Hannah was greatly inspired by Rose Kretsinger, a marvelous appliqué artist from Emporia, Lyon County, Kansas, whom she met about this time. She had no desire to copy any of Kretsinger's designs, but instead designed her own flower quilts. Her Basket of Roses Medallion quilt was shown in *Quilter's Newsletter* #109, and her Iris quilt was shown on the cover of *Quilter's Newsletter* #119.

Beginnings of an eighth quilt were found after her death in 1943. The borders were complete, but there were no drawings to indicate her plan for the central motif. It is unusual to do the borders first, but borders were a strong part of Hannah's quilts—an important frame for her appliqué—which she carried out with the same extraordinary precision and workmanship used on her center design.

Hannah designed, appliquéd, and marked for quilting, but sent her tops out to be quilted. Unfortunately, the quilter's name was not recorded, and therefore, proper recognition cannot be made. The quilting, however, compliments Hannah's beautiful appliqué. There are eighteen stitches to the inch.

Hannah refused to let any of her quilts be shown in public because she was concerned that someone might use her designs. However, in 1979 and 1980 her family allowed Hannah's Basket of Roses Medallion quilt to travel with the Kansas Quilt exhibit, thus giving the public an opportunity to appreciate Hannah's exceptional talent. The Cranes quilt was chosen to represent Kansas at Quilt Symposium '79 in California. An article, "My Great-Great Aunt Made Quilts" by Marie Shirer, appeared in the February 1980 issue of *Quilters Newsletter*. It tells the story of Hannah Haynes Headlee and shows four of her seven and a half quilts. The Cranes quilt is loved and cared for by Hannah's great-great-niece Kathy Webber.

Owned by Kathy Webber, Shelton.

STEVE VENTO PHOTOGRAPHY

1934
DOUBLE WEDDING RING

66" x 84"

ASELENA FAA OLSON DONELSON, quiltmaker

Aselena Faa Olson, affectionately called "Lena" by her family, was born October 20, 1858. She married at the age of fifteen and raised her family of three boys and one girl in Minnesota. After being widowed in 1908, she moved to Zillah, Yakima County, Washington, to be close to her son Elrick and his family. Both she and Elrick remained in Zillah for the rest of their lives.

Elrick's daughter Eleanor moved to Bellingham, Whatcom County, Washington, after marrying a young man named Mike Moren. She had two daughters, Mary Ann and Sally, who were born in Bellingham. Sally was special to her great-grandmother Lena because she was born on Lena's birthday. Lena made baby quilts and full-size quilts for each of the girls. The full-size Double Wedding Ring quilt was a gift to Sally, and the baby quilt was made for Mary Ann. How unusual to find a baby quilt made out of the Double Wedding Ring pattern in the 1930s. In the 1980s small wall quilts are made using this pattern, but traditionally, it is a wedding quilt not a baby quilt.

Lena was in her late seventies when she made these accurately pieced cotton quilts. She used scraps of calicos, florals, geometrics, ginghams, and plaid cottons. Note that the four patches joining the rings are also made from scraps, where most Double Wedding Ring quilts have matching solid-color, cotton four patches. Lena quilted these quilts with 1-inch diamond cross-hatching and outlined each side of the rings. The quilts are bound with muslin bias binding.

Full-size Double Wedding Ring owned by Sally Lindman. Small Double Wedding Ring owned by Nancy Cohen, Edmonds, the great-great granddaughter of Lena.

Lena Olson Donelson with her great-granddaughters: Sally in her arms and Mary Ann standing.

Double Wedding Ring, 1935, 40" x 42".

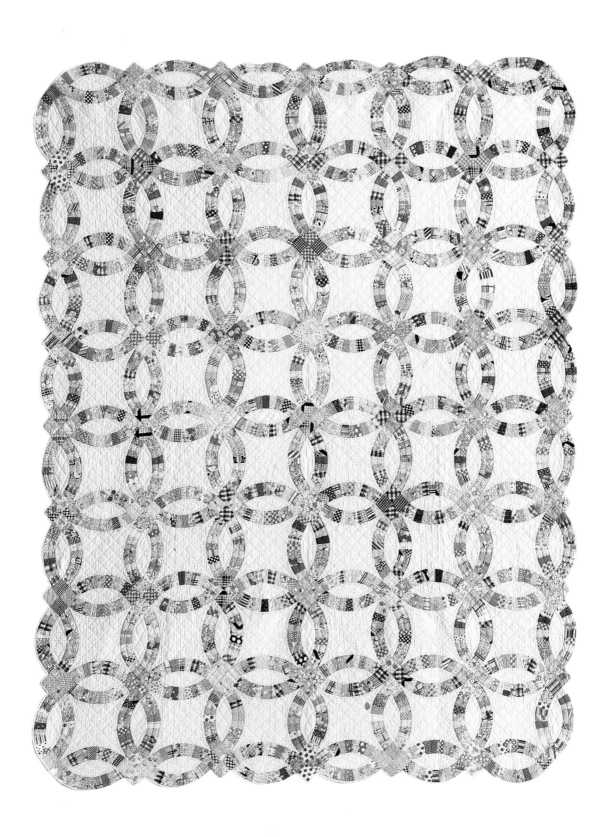

1935
STAR OF MANY POINTS

74″ x 94″

JESSIE JOHNSON BRADLEY PORTER, quiltmaker

Jessie Johnson was born April 8, 1869, to a very religious New England family. Her family moved to Riverside, Riverside County, California, in the 1880s. In 1887 Jessie married an artist and musician, Edward G. Bradley. Jessie and Edward had two children, Alfred and Ethel.

When Ethel was an infant, Edward left his wife and children in search of adventure and to fight in the Spanish American War. In his absence, Jessie supported herself and the two children by taking in sewing. Edward did not return for three years. When he finally walked in the door, unannounced, and proudly showed a large handful of gold coins to his family, Jessie was so angered that she brought her hand up under his, and the coins flew all over the kitchen.

In 1910 Edward wanted to move his family to Palo Alto, Santa Clara County, California, but Jessie refused. This strong woman was not going to let a man dictate her life. As a result, Jessie and Edward were divorced. Jessie continued to support her family by designing and making dresses for wealthy Southern California women. She invested money from her dress designing business and bought land and rental property. She was an active lady and enjoyed doing some kind of handwork whenever she sat down.

In the early 1930s Jessie married E. Y. Porter, an electrical engineer. During this time she gave up her dressmaking and turned to quiltmaking. Two of her quilts have been handed down through her daughter Ethel's family. The pattern for one of these quilts—the Star of Many Points—was taken from the newspaper. In 1936 Jessie gave this Star of Many Points quilt to Ethel, who was married and living in Washington State. Jessie asked that the quilt always be used, not stored away. In

Jessie Bradley Porter.

the 1950s when Ethel and Edward Twelker's son Al married Nancyann Johanson, a quilt lover, the quilt was passed onto them.

There are sixty-three 10½-inch blocks set 7 x 9. This all-cotton, blue and white quilt is beautifully hand quilted and bound with a double bias tape that Jessie made to match the quilt. On the back it is signed "Jessie E. Bradley-Porter Riverside Calif. 1935." The quilt was used continuously for fifty years until the binding began to show signs of wear. It is now on display in the Twelker home and accompanies Nancyann on many lectures about women and their quilts.

Collection of Alois and Nancyann Johanson Twelker, Seattle.

1938
ELEPHANT'S CHILD

77" x 94"

MINNIE PETERSON BJORK, quiltmaker

Minnie Bjork.

This hand-appliquéd quilt is based on one of Rudyard Kipling's *Just-So Stories,* The Elephant's Child. The design, by E. Buckner Kirk, appeared in a 1930s women's magazine. Minnie Bjork could not afford the $5 kit, so she drew the pattern herself from the photograph in the magazine. She used plaid, printed, and solid cottons for her appliqué, and a beautiful cotton sateen for the background. The quilting and finishing of the quilt took six weeks of daily work. Minnie entered the quilt in the Traverse County Fair in Wheaton, Minnesota, and won first place.

Minnie Elizabeth Peterson was born March 7, 1897. She married Orlando Bjork, and they had one child Joanne. Minnie began quilting in 1931. She made this Elephant's Child quilt for Joanne. During the Depression, she belonged to the Rosholt Quilting Club, which met any day, except Sunday, that a quilt was ready. The women would spend the whole day quilting, and toward evening, their husbands would join them for a supper, which everyone helped put together. For many of the ladies, this was their only time away from home during the week. They enjoyed quilting, visiting, and eating with one another. One year they finished fifty quilts. Minnie also made at least two quilts a year by herself. She shared her quilting stories with her grandchildren, relating how in the 1930s most good cotton cost around fifteen to twenty-five cents a yard. Once she bought forty yards of 80-count cotton on sale for six cents a yard. It was used for many quilts.

In addition to quilting, Minnie loved to share her Scandinavian heritage with her family. Each year she spent the time between Thanksgiving and Christmas baking and making Scandinavian treats, cookies, lefse, and potato sausage for Christmas smorgasbord.

By her death in 1986, Minnie had made special quilts for each of her eight grandchildren. Joanne Bjork Klein passed the Elephant's Child quilt on to her son Bob. When Bob married Cindy Mott in 1974 in Tacoma, Washington, Minnie gave them two quilts: an all-cotton Trip Around the World and a scrap quilt made of many fabrics. This small, energetic lady will long be remembered by her family and all who see her Elephant's Child quilt.

Owned by Bob and Cindy Klein, Everson.

The 1930s magazine illustration of the Elephant's Child quilt.

1940
GRANDMOTHER'S FAN

72½" x 98"

CLARA WEIL MITTENDORF WALKER, quiltmaker

Clara Weil Mittendorf Walker.

Clara Weil Mittendorf Walker made two identical fan quilts and gave them to her two grandchildren. This wonderful fan quilt has been in use ever since its completion. The colors are soft and lovely examples of 1930s cottons. The 1½-inch pieced borders are marvelous. Pieced borders of this kind were unusual at that time. This quilt has eighty-eight 8-inch blocks. Originally the back was brought to the front to bind the edge. In 1987 a bias binding was added to cover the frayed edges. The pattern for the quilt was taken from a Seattle, Washington, newspaper.

Clara's only child Jack Mittendorf remembers his mother, grandmother, and aunt sitting on the front porch quilting. They used quilt hoops. During World War II, Clara knitted over two thousand hours' worth of items for the American Red Cross. Clara was born January 21, 1895, in Philadelphia, Philadelphia County, Pennsylvania. Irwin Mittendorf was her first husband; Olin "Tex" Walker was her second. Clara died September 29, 1974, in Seattle, Washington.

Owned by Dan Mittendorf, Seattle.

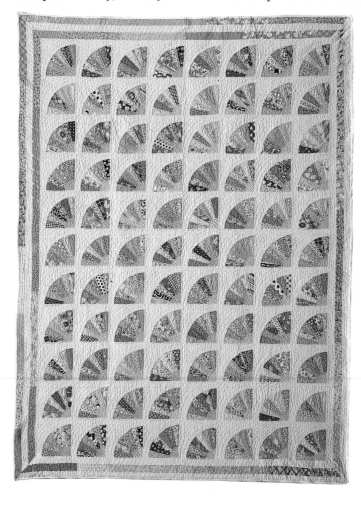

1940
LeMoyne Star Doll Quilt

31″ x 31½″

Pearl Mable Griffith
Humphrey, quiltmaker

❧ Pearl Mable Griffith Humphrey's niece Dotty Griffith loved to play with dolls. When she was nine years old she received a gift of a doll bed and newly made doll clothes. Aunt Pearl sent along this hand-pieced and hand-quilted doll quilt for the new doll bed. The small 6-inch blocks are made from cotton scraps and a solid blue cotton. The background is white broadcloth and has matching handmade bias binding. The quilting stitches outline the pieces. The quilt has occupied the same doll bed all of its life. Dotty has her doll, doll bed, and doll quilt sitting in a corner of her living room in Edmonds, Snohomish County, Washington.

In the late 1960s Dotty became interested in quilting. She wrote and asked Aunt Pearl about quilting. Pearl sent her a box of patterns, samples, instructions, and a lot of encouragement. Dotty quilted her first quilt in a frame made from four 1 x 3s and four clamps. The frame was supported by chair backs. Pearl commented that Dotty was going to think she was quilting Puget Sound before she finished. It was a full-size quilt and a large "first" project.

Pearl was born September 6, 1891, near Ritzville, Adams County, Washington. Pearl was one of twelve children, of whom only nine—three girls and six boys—survived. The girls all learned to stitch and do the

Margret Jane, Pearl Mable, and Edith Christina Griffith.

domestic chores allotted to women at that time. The photograph shows all three girls: Pearl in the back, Margret on the left, and Edith on the right. Pearl married Lyle Humphrey in Spokane, Spokane County, Washington, September 23, 1908. They had five children. The family lived on a farm in the Spokane area. Pearl made many quilts, some from patterns out of the *Farm Journal*. She crocheted and did many of the needle arts. She even made an embroidered quilt record of several generations of family names. She entered county fairs and received many blue ribbons.

Pearl and Lyle lived to celebrate their sixtieth wedding anniversary. Pearl died January 1, 1974, in Spokane. Dotty still quilts, belongs to several quilting groups, and enjoys sitting at her modern quilting frame in front of her window that looks out on Puget Sound. She misses Aunt Pearl, the special bond they had, and their mutual interest in quilting.

Collection of Dotty Griffith Charlson, Edmonds.

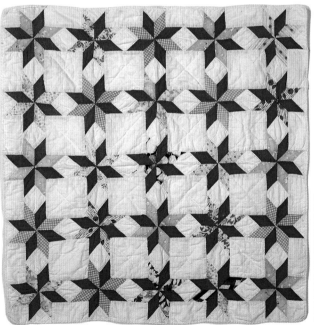

CARL MURRAY PHOTOGRAPHY

1954
CRACKER BOX

50" x 80"

BERNICE "BEA" IRENE RILEY SMALLEY, quiltmaker

These quilts were made at a time when quiltmaking was at a low ebb in Washington State and throughout the country. Many women in Washington State had taken defense jobs during World War II and continued to work through the Korean War. In the Pacific Northwest there were many defense industries that provided job opportunities for women and, in fact, with the shortage of men, women were needed to fill these jobs.

Bernice Irene Riley was born October 6, 1914 in Ashland, Clark County, Kansas. Bea always enjoyed needlework. When she was twelve years old, she was invited to quilt with the ladies group at the Christian Church in Coldwater, Kansas. She joined them weekly. She taught herself how to piece and did so whenever she had time. It became a way of life. She married Russell "Dick" Smalley on Christmas Eve in 1935. They had three daughters, DeLayne, Sherry Beth, and Shirley Ann. In 1948 the family moved to the Tacoma area, Pierce County, Washington.

Bernice "Bea" Riley Smalley.

Bea's mother Della Currier Riley was piecing Cracker Box when she died in 1952 at the age of sixty-two in Tacoma, Washington. Bea finished the piecing, set the forty 10-inch blocks together, and quilted. The Cracker Box pattern is from a 1930s Women's World magazine. The quilt has been saved ever since as a legacy of quilting from mother to daughter.

Bea made the Bow Tie quilt in 1948. The blocks are 8-inches square and set on the diagonal with alternating unpieced blocks. Usually the blocks are set on the straight without lattice or alternating blocks. Bow Tie quilts are frequently made from many different fabrics—a great scrap quilt. This pattern is traditionally made for a male member of the family.

Bea continues to enjoy the art of quilting. Her stitches are small, even, and straight. She takes great pride in her work. Bea quilts five days a week at her local senior citizen center to help support the center. She arrives shortly after 8 A.M. and quilts on a full-size, old-style frame until lunchtime. The frame is set up in the corner windows of the center, and people walking by stop to watch and come in to visit and see what Bea is working on. Seeing Bea quilting brings back many family memories to people at the center. After lunch Bea goes home to the farm and quilts in a hoop for herself and her family.

Owned by Bernice Riley Smalley, Roy.

Bow Tie, 1948, 68" x 78".

1977
GROUCHO MARX MEMORIAL QUILT

86" x 92"

MARTHA FORBES HOLLINGSWORTH and
JANA CLAIRE HOLLINGSWORTH, quiltmakers

❧ Martha Forbes Hollingsworth and Jana Claire Hollingsworth are a lovely mother/daughter team; they do many wonderful things together, one of which is quilting. In particular, they enjoy planning the quilts that they make, either individually or together. They go to breakfast, lunch, or dinner to talk out their ideas, making notes and sketching on scratch paper, napkins, tablecloths, or whatever is available when the creative thoughts begin to rush. A product of such brainstorming is the Groucho Marx Memorial Quilt or "How would you like to come up to my place and read my bed?" Martha and Jana are both Groucho fans, and they planned this quilt as a tribute to Groucho's many years of entertaining.

The Groucho Marx Memorial quilt was designed with Higgins India ink on white cotton fabric and, in part, with the use of a light table. The quilting was done by hand. The pictures from Groucho's movies are all different. The quilt received the Best of Show award in the 1978 Fiberwork Show, Port Townsend, Washington, as well as an award in the 1979 Edmonds Art Festival. It appeared in the Port Angeles Arts in Action Show in 1980 and was accepted for the Bellevue Art Festival in 1981.

Martha was born April 21, 1924, in Skykomish, King County, Washington, in the railroad car that her family

Martha Hollingsworth and Jana Hollingsworth.

was living in while her father worked as a civil engineer laying railroad track for logging companies. Martha received a degree in journalism from the University of Washington and wrote a column for the Seattle Star until her marriage to Clar Hollingsworth in 1950. Clar owned and operated a Dental Laboratory in Port Angeles, Clallam County, Washington, until his retirement in 1987. Martha works as a church secretary and belongs to a local quilt group. Jana was born February 5, 1954, in Port Angeles, Washington. She is a professional cartographer. Map making enables her to combine her background in political science and geography with her artistic abilities.

Another of Jana's prominent creations is the H.M.S. Pinafore Centennial Quilt, which is based on the Gilbert and Sullivan opera. It is made with a wide range of rich, lush fabrics, much in the style of a Victorian crazy quilt.

Jana is currently working on her third panel for the San Francisco AIDS memorial quilt, a project that promotes the need for AIDS research and serves as a memorial to AIDS victims. Jana, a caring, loving woman, combines her concern and love for friends and neighbors with her artistic and needle expertise.

Collection of Martha Forbes Hollingsworth and Jana Claire Hollingsworth, Port Angeles.

1981
THE SUN'S GARDEN

77" x 110"

JOANNE S. HALDEMAN, quiltmaker

JoAnne Selman was born March 28, 1927, in Buhl, Twin Falls County, Idaho. She majored in art at the University of California in Los Angeles and attended the Chaunard School of Design only to decide that she was not interested in fashion design, but rather in painting with oils and watercolors.

In 1948 JoAnne married Don Haldeman. A year later they moved to Washington State. They have two sons and a daughter. After her marriage, JoAnne continued to paint and to teach both painting and stitchery. From 1960 to 1961 she was president of Women Painters of Washington. She was also a charter member of the Pacific Northwest Needle Arts Guild.

In the mid sixties JoAnne started to work more and more with fibers until work with fabric became her specialty. Eventually she became a quilt designer and quiltmaker, and she has been teaching quilting in the greater Seattle area since 1976. JoAnne enjoys working with a variety of techniques, from the quickly assembled seminole quilts she made for her children to the reverse appliqué quilts, whose patterns are so popular with her students.

All of her quilts reflect an exceptional use and sense of color. Using the Kaleidoscope pattern, she creates entirely different quilts that often cannot be recognised as the traditional pattern. Her use of color is the important key.

The Sun's Garden—a painting in fabric—grew until JoAnne contained the garden with a quilted fence border. Each flower is hand pieced. JoAnne drew them on paper and then cut apart the paper to use as the patterns. The borders are machine pieced. JoAnne quilts in a hoop, and the quilting follows the design of the piecing. The background quilting is cross-hatching. The backing fabric was brought to the front to form the frame (binding) for this fabric painting.

Collection of artist JoAnne S. Haldeman, Kirkland.

JoAnne S. Haldeman

1982
Roses on the Fence
90″ x 90″

Dorothy "Dottie" Jenstad
Pedersen, quiltmaker

Dorothy "Dottie" Pedersen.

Dorothy "Dottie" Jenstad was born April 3, 1921, in Fargo, Cass County, North Dakota. She loved to ride her bicycle all around town and was on one such ride when she met Peter Beyer Pedersen. They were married January 3, 1941, in Fargo, Cass County, North Dakota. In April of 1942 they moved to Seattle, King County, Washington, where three months later, Beyer was drafted into the Army Air Corps. Dottie and Beyer had two children, Bradley, born in 1949, and Margaret Anne, born in 1952. Before retiring in 1976, Dottie was active with a job and various clubs.

As a young girl, Dottie had embroidered flowers on triangular pieces of muslin, which when joined with a pieced triangle would form a Basket of Flowers quilt. The embroidery designs were from the Fargo, North Dakota, newspaper. The embroidery was all finished and neatly packed in a box. The piecing never happened. It was not until she retired that Dottie took her first patchwork and quilting class. She had always enjoyed sewing and doing all forms of needlework. That class was the start of an all-consuming passion, which became the focal point of her life. She joined Quilter's Anonymous of Edmonds, the Pacific Northwest Needle Arts Guild, belonged to Needle and I, and was a Wednesday Friendship quilter. Dottie always had projects in progress. She took workshops,

went to quilting retreats, quilt and needlework conferences, and applied everything she learned. She completed four full-size quilts, four crib-size quilts, and numerous wall-size quilts plus quilted clothing and other items. She was exact in her piecing and appliqué and had wonderfully small, straight, and even stitches.

Even after being diagnosed with cancer in the fall of 1984, Dottie still found much joy in life and continued to love stitching. When she could no longer stitch, she still wanted her quilt group to come to her house so she could listen and watch everyone around the frame. Her dear friends in Idaho sent her a Rose of Sharon quilt to keep her warm and make her feel especially loved. Her memorial service in June of 1985 was a wonderful one-woman show. All of her quilts were displayed in the church.

Dottie called her Log Cabin quilt, Roses on the Fence, because of the rose border print, which adds elegance to the warm pink and beige cabin colors. It has 64 blocks set 8 x 8, not a common set for a log cabin. If you look carefully at the design, you can see four large stars. The quilt is machined pieced and hand quilted. Each log is hand quilted with short, straight, and precise stitches. Roses on the Fence won many awards throughout Washington State.

Owned by Margaret Anne Pedersen Myers, Monroe.

1983
KILAUEA IKI
96″ x 96″

HELEN ORTQUIST DYER, quiltmaker

Helen Ortquist Dyer.

Helen Ortquist Dyer was born March 31, 1920, in Montesano, Grays Harbor County, Washington, where she lived for the first eighteen years of her life. Helen's parents were emigrants from Sweden, and she grew up under influences of the old country. As a sickly pre-schooler she learned embroidery and spent much of her time doing stitchery. Her mother, who had studied stitchery in Sweden, made wool comforters. Helen's only exposure to quiltmaking as a child came from a neighbor who made patchwork quilts. She remembers being fascinated by the Double Wedding Ring quilt design.

One day when their parents were not at home, one of Helen's older brothers taught her how to use their mother's treadle sewing machine. Helen was eight years old at the time. With this new skill she spent several years making doll clothes. On her twelfth birthday, her oldest brother gave her dress fabric and a pattern; this was the beginning of a lifetime of sewing for herself and others. Her parents considered sewing to be a worthwhile hobby and permitted her to do as much as she liked. She soon discovered that she could make something new every week. Weekly projects became a goal that she carried through all her life, until she became hooked on quilting.

Helen's interests took her to the Charette School of Design in Seattle, Washington. After graduating, she stayed on as an instructor. In 1942 she went to Portland, Oregon, as the director of the branch school. Three years later she met and married first lieutenant Kenneth Layton Dyer, Jr., of the U.S. Army Air Corps. Among the numerous places they were stationed during her husband's thirty years in the service was Hawaii. It was there, at the Bishop Museum in 1958, that she was exposed to Hawaiian quilting for the first time. She enrolled in two different series of classes from Mealii Kalama. Her first original pattern design was a Bird of Paradise. It was not completed until 1975, the same year it won a blue ribbon at the Western Washington State Fair. Since then Helen has won many ribbons, including more than twenty blue ribbons at fairs and shows.

Kilauea Iki is an adaptation of a Hawaiian pattern called Volcano. The red fabric represents the fire, and the background represents lava. The border represents fissure-type eruptions, while the extreme center shows the lava flowing back into the original crater. Both Kilauea Iki, on the big island of Hawaii, and Mount Saint

Helens in Gifford Pinchot National Forest, Cowlitz County, Washington, erupted while Helen was working on this magnificent quilt. Helen finds Hawaiian quilting the most exciting form of all quiltmaking. She quilts these large projects in a hoop. Helen also enjoys working her original designs on small projects. Helen had the honor of being the only mainlander invited to display her Hawaiian quilts at the 1984 Kahala Quilt Show in Hawaii.

Collection of Helen Ortquist Dyer, Seattle

Bird of Paradise, 1969, 97″ x 102″.

1985
GARDEN PATH

48″ x 65″

MARION RAY REID, quiltmaker

Marion Ray Reid.

Marion Ray Reid's grandfather, Ray, came to Tacoma, Pierce County, Washington, in 1880, and established the Ray Printing Company. His son Alvis helped with the business. Alvis and his wife Frances had five daughters: Marion, Dixy, Jean, Juliana, and Alvista. Marion, who was born in 1913, first asked for a needle and thread when she was two years old. She has been using them ever since. Marion knits, crochets, does needlepoint, crewel work, sews garments and quilts. She remembers helping her grandmother with quilts.

Marion grew up helping her mother with her four younger sisters. She attended the College of Puget Sound, Tacoma, Washington, and the University of Redlands, Redlands, California. She married Gordon Reid, and they had three children. Gordon died at the Ray family farm on Fox Island, Washington, in December 1974. They had been married thirty-seven years. Marion, who had always been very active with family and community affairs, did not slow down after Gordon's death. She continued to run the family farm and to be involved with the people around her.

In 1976, when her sister Dixy decided to run for governor of Washington State, Marion became treasurer of the campaign. As a result of Marion's administrative abilities, Dixy Lee Ray was the first elected official of this state to take office debt free. Marion served as a most gracious first lady. She managed the Governor's Mansion, served on committees, kept abreast of all current events, took care of the farm, and still found time to work on her stamp collection and to stitch.

Since retiring from public life, this wonderfully kind, truthful, gentle but firm lady lives on the family farm. She is active in the Fox Island Historical Society and Museum and is the founder of Stitch and Bitch, a group of women that meets bimonthly to stitch and discuss matters of importance.

The Garden Path or Rail Fence quilt is an attractive variation of a traditional pattern. There are forty-two 6½-inch blocks set 6 x 7. This quilt has been handquilted in the ditch through a fat batting to give the overall appearance of a comforter. In the lower right-hand block the quilt is signed, "Marion R. Reid, 1985."

Owned by Marion Ray Reid, Fox Island.

STEVE VENTO PHOTOGRAPHY

1985
MINIATURE PAISLEY JEWELS

89″ x 89″

ELDRA PICKERING JONES
PEBSWORTH, quiltmaker

Eldra Pickering was born September 12, 1912, in Seattle, King County, Washington, and has lived in Washington all her life. Eldra has been twice widowed, has two children, and has led an active life. When she retired from the State Department of Social and Health Services in 1974, she had already made one hundred quilts. She decided it was time to stop counting, but kept on quilting.

Eldra has a marvelous fabric library. This special collection includes her favorite—the paisley design. This fabric library fills her garage, which has been converted into a storage area just to house the fabric. In addition to her outstanding collection of fabric, Eldra has collected quilt patterns. She has clipped patterns from newspapers and magazines and has purchased quilt books. Her interest has kept her informed and up-to-date on fabrics, patterns, and techniques.

Her hands are always busy, and if she is not quilting, she is knitting. She knits tiny booties and makes lightweight quilts for a local hospital's ward for premature babies, knits special wool socks for several diabetics, and shares her quilting expertise with all who ask. She is the sweetheart of several quilt groups. Her quilt was named by her daughter Sylvia who thought all the miniature paisley hexagons sparkled like jewels. This quilt is all hand pieced and quilted and was expertly constructed—it lies absolutely flat.

Collection of Sylvia Jones Bartow, Seattle.

Eldra Pebsworth.

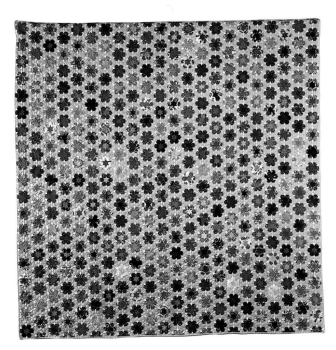

Quilt patterns from newspapers of the 1930s.

1986
HEARTS AND CRYSTALS
70" x 70"

SALLIE JEANNETTE WILSON
LINGWOOD, quiltmaker

Sallie Wilson Lingwood.

Sallie Jeannette Wilson was born August 18, 1916, on a homestead near Terry, Prairie County, Montana. Sallie's mother became seriously ill when Sallie was only two years old. Sallie and her younger sister Lois were cared for by women on the surrounding homesteads. When Sallie was four years old one woman gave her a piece of cloth and a needle and thread. Her first stitching was a pillowslip for her doll. On Christmas of 1922 Sallie received a brown sewing box containing yellow cloth, thread, needle, and a thimble.

In January 1923 Sallie and Lois went to live with their father's loving parents and family in North Carolina. Sallie's grandmother Sallie Ann Wilson and her aunts were all very fine stitchers. They made quilts frequently—some of wool, some of cotton. The quilts were used on the family beds. Sallie watched and learned. When she was ten and eleven years old she made her first quilt top using fabric from the family scrap bag.

In 1928 Sallie moved West to live with her mother's aunt and uncle in Anacortes, Skagit County, Washington. Her aunt was pleased to have Sallie and encouraged her interest in the needle arts. Sallie helped her aunt and friends piece and quilt. One lady, Ruby Raddatz, took extra time to show Sallie how to make small, even, and straight stitches. While Sallie was in high school she pieced and quilted several quilts. One quilt, Noonday Lily, was made for a Seattle lady, who paid her $10 for it. At seventeen, Sallie pieced and quilted a Pine Tree quilt, which won an award at the state fair. The fabric for the Pine Tree quilt was purchased at J. C. Penney's for twenty-nine cents a yard.

In 1942 Sallie married a Seattle man, Ralph Lingwood, in the Old Methodist Church in Anacortes, Washington. They moved to Elmhurst, DuPage County, Illinois, where they lived with their two daughters, Sara Anne and Dianna Jean. After Ralph died in 1959, Sallie returned to Anacortes with her daughters. She had a home-operated gingerbread cookie business and spent many hours on her needlework. She quilted, made clothing, and did petit point. Sallie's work "Poppies" won awards at a 1976 exhibit in Monaco held by the American Needlepoint Guild at the invitation of Princess Grace.

Sallie's blue-and-white Hearts and Crystals, a Sisters Choice variation, won two awards in 1986. This remark-able quilt has fancy feathered hearts quilted in the unpieced blocks and in the white border, and a heart vine design quilted in the blue border. The quilting is every ¼ inch to ½ inch over the entire surface with blue outline stitch embroidered on hearts and on the country-blue border, done to accent the quilting.

Sallie lives in a marvelous, large old home in Anacortes, Washington, called the Nantucket Inn, where one can rent a room for the night. She quilts evenings while her guests enjoy her hospitality. Sallie quilts without benefit of hoop or frame, and her needle flies, making tiny precise stitches.

From the collection of Sallie Jeannette Wilson Lingwood, Anacortes.

1986
THE IMMIGRANTS
72" x 72"
JANICE OHLSON RICHARDS, quiltmaker

The Immigrants was designed for the Great American Quilt Contest that celebrated the centennial of the Statue of Liberty in 1986. It was made with much feeling as artist Janice Ohlson Richards expresses: "The statue, itself, stands as a symbol of liberty and hope, and in designing the quilt, I wanted to try to capture the moment they (the immigrants) set their eyes on it—that feeling. Our country's rich heritage is due, in part, to those brave immigrants, leaving family behind to search for a new life in America. Their dress intrigued me, and I tried to portray this when selecting fabric; the dark coats, trousers with suspenders, and bouskas over the women's hair. My grandfather came over from Sweden in 1903 at age sixteen."

Janice used many fabrics in this quilt, including: corduroy, satin, polished cotton, and calico. The blond man represents her grandfather. The immigrants are standing in the bow of the ship, seeing the Statue of Liberty for the first time. Janice machine pieced her quilt, then hand quilted it with small, straight, and even stitches. She quilts using a hoop. The bias binding is handmade. The quilt receives awards wherever it is shown in Washington State.

Janice was born September 20, 1939, in Tacoma, Pierce County, Washington. She graduated from the University of Washington. She married William Gordon, and they raised two children on Fox Island, Pierce County, Washington, where she continues to live. It is this environment that spurs her creativity. The windows of her home look over tree tops to the waters of Puget Sound. Her studio looks out onto a lovely flower garden backed by evergreen trees.

Janice has always enjoyed working with her hands. She learned embroidery, crocheting, and sewing at an early age from her mother and grandmother. Her interest in quiltmaking began in 1977 when she took a class through the Tacoma Parks Department. Since then she has taken workshops from nationally known artists and has discovered that fiber is a wonderful way to express her ideas. These ideas have found their way into wearable-art vests and jackets as well as quilts. Most of her quilts fall into the category of contemporary, geometric pieced designs, but her work knows no bounds.

Collection of artist Janice Ohlson Richards, Fox Island.

Janice Ohlson Richards.

1987
Basket Medallion

83″ x 100″

Donna Hanson Eines, quiltmaker

This marvelously original Basket Medallion quilt has added many blue ribbons to Donna Hanson Eines growing collection. In this quilt, Donna used three sizes of pieced baskets, four different basket patterns, and a pieced and appliquéd basket border for the top and bottom. Donna took a favorite traditional pattern, set it in an untraditional manner, and made it a masterpiece with exquisite quilting. Her quilting stitches are so very close and fine that the unquilted portion of the quilting design appears to be stuffed.

Donna, who does most of her quilting in a hoop, loves to have a lot of quilting on her quilts, and she does not care how much time is spent achieving the desired look. It is part of the loving legacy she wants to leave her family.

Donna was born in 1930 in Seattle, King County, Washington. She married Ivar Eines in 1950. They raised their family in Edmonds, Snohomish County, Washington. Sewing was Donna's hobby from grade school on, until it fell by the wayside when she became interested in quilting. She credits her sister-in-law Marie Hellyer for introducing her to the world of quilts. At first Donna spent a year reading about the art of quiltmaking. She loved the history and folksy tales of women in the early pioneer days, and she thoroughly appreciated the visual concept, graphic design, color interplay, and texture of quilts. Finally, she chose Cathedral Window as her first project, because it did not require a quilting frame. She completed Cathedral Window in a year and a half. It won two awards at the Island County Fair on Whidbey Island, Washington, in 1975. Since this first project, quilting has become an all-consuming way of life for Donna. She has completed fourteen full-size quilts, fifteen wall quilts, and has more in progress. Several of her designs have been published.

Donna Hanson Eines.

Donna is an active member of several quilting groups, including the Wednesday Friendship Quilters. Donna's appreciation of all kinds of needlework is reflected in the cross-stitch samplers and framed quilt pieces that decorate her home. When not quilting, Donna loves visiting antique shops to look for quilts and darning eggs. She has an outstanding and unusual collection of darners.

Collection of Donna Hanson Eines, Edmonds.

Ribbons won by Donna Eines for her quilts.

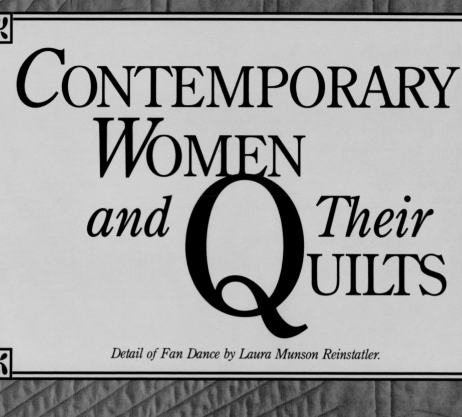

CONTEMPORARY
WOMEN
and QTheir QUILTS

Detail of Fan Dance by Laura Munson Reinstatler.

Quilts are in the artist's collection unless otherwise noted.

Winter Survival/Affirmation Coat, 61″ x
45″. Mary Preston, Tacoma, © 1987. Hand
painted, machine quilted, embellished with
painted yarn and beads.

The Mountain is Out, 78″ x 90″. Joan Wolfrom,
© 1985. Machine pieced and quilted. Owned by Dr. and
Mrs. William Wilbert, Gig Harbor.

Fan Dance, 52″ x 52½″. Laura Munson Reinstatler,
Mill Creek, © 1986. Machine pieced and quilted.

Art History Series–Classical Greek, 40" x 48" x 2". Margaret Hayes, Lynnwood, ©1986. Fabric relief sculpture, hand sewn, hand quilted. (Photograph by Richard Hayes)

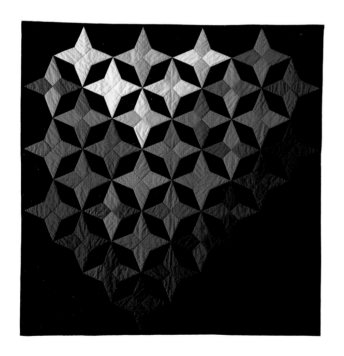

Starry Amish Night, 56" x 56". Judy Sogn, Seattle, ©1987. Machine pieced and hand quilted.

Cascade Summer, 56" x 56". Bonnie Mitchell, Everett, ©1987. Washington State blocks, hand and machine pieced, hand quilted.

Reflecting ... with Reflections, 82" x 82". Karen Schoepflin Hagen, Richland, © 1984. Hand appliquéd and quilted.

Night Train to Hong Kong, 46″ x 53″. Donna Pritchard, Bellevue, © 1986. Pieced kimono, couched cords, edges of pieces are dry brush painted. (Photograph by Eduardo Calderon)

English Ivy, 85″ x 101″. Joyce Bennion Peaden, Prosser, © 1986. Quilted by Buena Heights Quilters, © 1987.

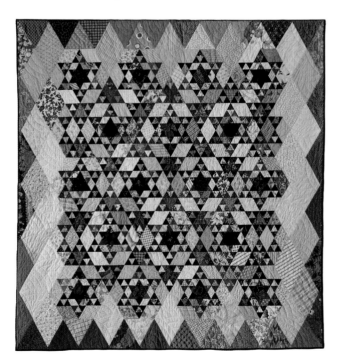

Stars as Seen from the Forest Floor, 80″ x 84″. Annette Anderson, Deming, © 1988. Hand pieced and quilted.

Northwest Bear, 80″ x 97″. Joyce Pennington, Edmonds, © 1982. Hand appliquéd, hand quilted. (Photograph by Carl Murray)

Pond Life, 90″ x 110″. Suzanne Hammond, Bellingham, © 1986. Machine pieced and quilted.

Evergreen Village, 76″ x 84″. Mary Hickey, Seattle, © 1986. Machine pieced, hand quilted. (Photograph by Carl Murray)

Seminole Sampler Square Dancing Costume, Lassie Wittman, Rochester, © 1982. Machine Seminole piecing. (Photograph by Beverly Rush)

The Annapolis Mariner, 92″ x 102″. Joyce Schaberg Miller, Edmonds, © 1986. Hand pieced and quilted. Owned by Karen Miller Ebersole. (Photograph by Carl Murray)

Feathered Star Sampler, 76″ x 76″. Marsha McCloskey, Seattle, © 1985. Machine pieced, hand quilted.

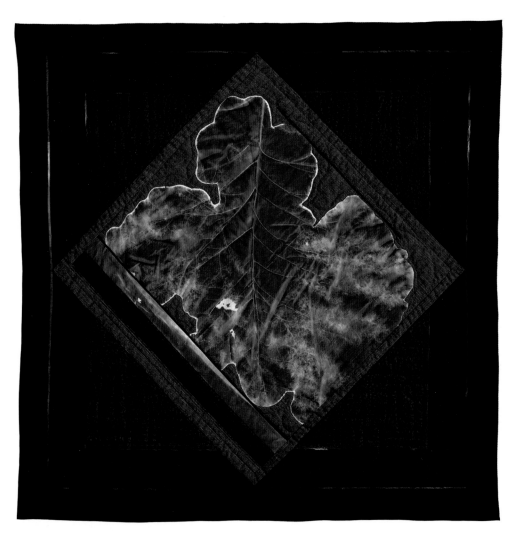

Reflections in My Mobile World, 60″ x 60″. Betty Ferguson, Richland, © 1986. Machine pieced, hand quilted.

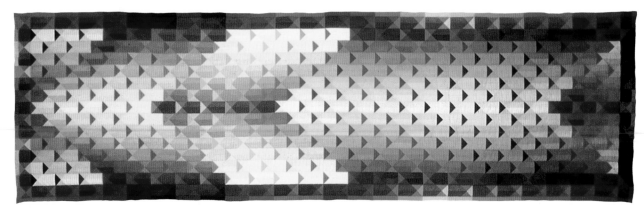

Light Year, 13′ x 3′10″. Suzanne Kjelland, Gig Harbor, © 1985. Hand-dyed cotton, machine quilted. (Photograph by Ken Wagner)

Fly Away Free, 60″ x 48″. Nancy Dice, Bellevue, © 1987. Hand and machine pieced, appliquéd, embroidered, hand quilted.

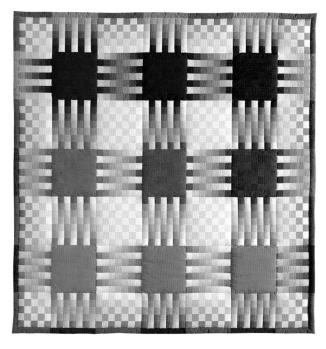

Starry Night, 60″ x 60″. Suzanne Kjelland, Gig Harbor, © 1986. Hand-dyed cotton, machine quilted. (Photograph by Ken Wagner)

Hexagon Flower Garden, 57″ x 72″. Reynola Pakusich, Bellingham, © 1987. Paper pieced. Hand quilted by Hazel Montague.

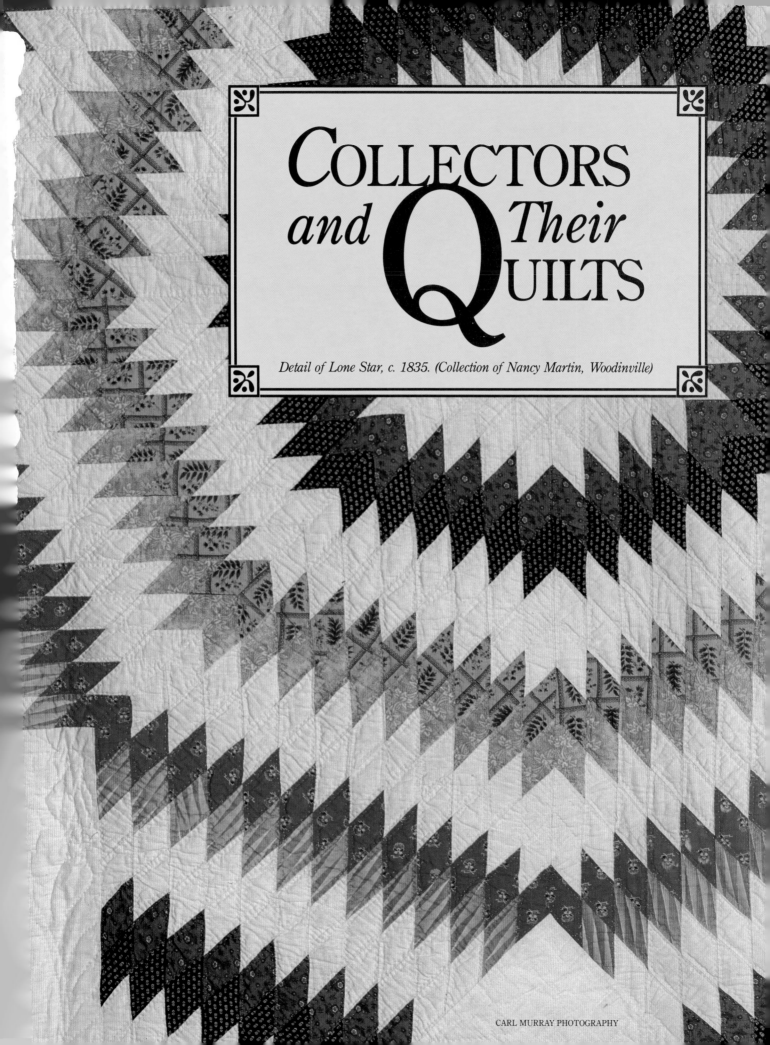

COLLECTORS and QTheir QUILTS

Detail of Lone Star, c. 1835. (Collection of Nancy Martin, Woodinville)

CARL MURRAY PHOTOGRAPHY

FELICIA MELERO HOLTZINGER

Quilt Collector

❈ Felicia Melero Holtzinger acquired her first quilt when she graduated from Yakima High School. A gift from her grandmother, Lillie May Taylor Bowen, this wonderful Log Cabin quilt was made by her great-grandmother Sarah Ann Schultz Taylor in 1915. Felicia's mother Vivian Pauline Bowen was born in Washington State and married Felix Melero, a Basque sheepherder who came to the Yakima Valley in the early 1920s.

Felicia's discerning eye has amassed a wonderful treasure of quilts and other collectibles in her Yakima home. Located in the center of an apple orchard, the house abounds with visual delights. Felicia's unique style and love of decorating is apparent throughout her home. As one enters the foyer, several collections are on display: an armoire full of antique quilts, a collection of dolls and miniature quilts displayed on doll-size furniture and trunks, china and glassware in glass-fronted cabinets and handsome beaded bags. Other collections, including folk art and pottery, are found throughout her antique-filled home.

Quilts are part of the lavish decorating scheme throughout the house, and the balcony above the foyer serves as an ever-changing gallery according to the season. Felicia began collecting quilts in the late 1970s. Her collection contains excellent samples of crib, pieced, wool, folk art, appliqué, and crazy quilts, as well as unquilted tops. At one time, Felicia tried limiting her collection to just patchwork quilts pieced from the pink, brown, and green fabrics of the late nineteenth century, but she found herself constantly being tempted by great finds that did not fit this narrow category.

Felicia's quilt collection is evenly comprised of local acquisitions and those she seeks out when traveling. Their sources range from local flea markets and swap meets to some of the country's top dealers.

This generous lady allows her quilts to be displayed at community events and by the Yakima Valley Museum and Historical Association.

TRACY FRENCH MCHUGH

Quilt Collector

Tracy took her first quiltmaking classes in 1976 and knew then that quilts and quilting were an American folk art that she wanted to collect and help preserve. She began by letting family members know that she wanted to have as many of the family quilts as they would entrust to her care. Tracy's maternal great-grandmother was a quilter, and some of her quilts had survived. This was the beginning of her documented collection.

In 1981 Tracy married Mick McHugh. Her enthusiasm for quilts got Mick interested, too. They enjoy searching for quilts. Once, while in Pennsylvania Amish country, they turned down a lane marked "Toys for Sale." While talking with the Amish gentleman, Tracy mentioned quilts. The man told them of his sister, a quilter, and offered to take them to see her. The drive in the McHugh's car was the Amish man's first automobile ride. His sister's home had many quilts, cupboardsful. She also had a collection of antique fabrics. The McHughs commissioned her to make them a traditional Amish quilt using antique fabrics. She finished the quilt, a Nine Patch set on point, in approximately six months.

Tracy loves scrap quilts and some contemporary quilts, but mostly she enjoys antique quilts. Tracy and Mick have three, small, beautiful and energetic daughters, who already point out quilts to their parents, and who enjoy the feel of their mother's antique quilts.

Nancy J. Martin

Quilt Collector

As an author, teacher, and president of That Patchwork Place, Nancy J. Martin has many opportunities to travel and seek out quilts. Her collection contains antique quilts made between 1835 and 1910 and many lovely old fabrics. Although Nancy claims to specialize in red and green or red and white quilts, she usually buys any quilt that fits her criteria: "a quilt that makes my heart sing."

Nancy has found many of her quilts in Pennsylvania, her native state. Each trip to visit family and friends includes a quilt tour or search, where special quilts or new-found friends usually result.

While in a flea market in Shupps Grove, Pennsylvania, in May of 1987, Nancy happened upon a couple trying to sell a family quilt to a vendor. Nancy watched the transaction and offered appropriate comments and was delighted when an agreement could not be reached. She made a better offer and carried away the magnificent Lone Star quilt (110 inches by 120 inches) displayed here, which dates back to 1835.

Nancy has decorated her home with many of her quilts; there are quilts on the walls, on the beds, folded in and on antique furniture, and displayed in many unusual and traditional ways. A visit to her home is like a walk through a quilter's dream. Every room is color coordinated and decorated down to the smallest detail. It is not unusual for Nancy to come up with a new way of decorating or displaying her quilts and to accomplish it within hours. This busy, creative woman abounds with energy and enthusiasm, and she shares her excitement about new finds with all around her.

CARL MURRAY PHOTOGRAPHY

ROSALIE PFEIFER

Quilt Collector

From an early age Rosalie was surrounded by family members who enjoyed sewing. It was only natural that she would appreciate all forms of textiles. Her quilt collecting started in the 1970s as a tool for lectures and for teaching quiltmaking. Her collection includes examples from the early 1800s to the 1980s. She uses her quilts and displays them throughout her home. Her special interest is the use of wool in patchwork and quilting, which her in-depth collection reflects.

Not only does Rosalie collect wool quilts but she also makes them. A favorite is an embroidered quilt made from her son Jack's Marine uniforms. She is always asked to bring this quilt to her lectures or her public displays. People remember it, identify with it, and enjoy seeing it time and time again.

The "Castle Gown" that Rosalie is wearing in the photograph was designed and sewn by Rosalie. It is of wool tweed, which she bought in Ireland.

Rosalie was born in Maryland, is a graduate of the Maryland Institute of Fine Arts, and has lived in Washington State for the last thirty years. She is active in several quilt groups, enjoys networking with other quiltmakers, and loves the search for still another wool quilt.

DIANA SCHMIDT

Quilt Collector

Diana Schmidt bought her first quilt in 1978 from her husband's client. The client had just sold her home, was moving, and wanted to sell her quilt.

The following year, while Diana was working in her studio and gift shop, Fifth Avenue Village, Yakima, Washington, a customer told her of a garage sale that had several quilts. Diana immediately closed her shop and rushed to the garage sale. She purchased five quilts for $95. Her favorite, a very graphic red, white, and blue star quilt hangs on a wall in her home. This great buy just started Diana's interest in collecting quilts.

Today, Diana's home is full of quilts and other textiles. There are quilts on the walls, over furniture, on beds and in a marvelous six-foot-tall antique glass cabinet with glass shelves, which beautifully displays more many-colored quilts. Her favorites are quilts with strong color contrast, such as her red, white, and blue quilts. Diana's friends have made miniature patchwork pillows to sit on the seats of her collection of miniature chairs and settees.

Diana has pieced her first quilt, a blue and white double Irish Chain, and is now handquilting it in a hoop.

Diana, an artist, is well known for her watercolors. Her work is noted for its cheerful subjects, use of color, and attention to detail. Her subjects range from the home and garden, pets, rooms and people, antiques, and quilts. Her professional art degree is from the University of Oregon. She has won many awards in both illustration and fine art. She has been featured in *Country Living* magazine's "Country Classics."

ANN LOUISE STOHL

Quilt Collector

In 1979 Ann bought her first quilt. With that purchase, she discovered that quilt collecting was not like antique collecting. When she found the right antique to fit a particular space in her home, she no longer had a desire for another of the same. But you can never have enough quilts; there is always another one to include in your collection.

Ann opened her shop, Ann Louise Fabric and Folkart, in Yakima, Washington, in 1982. Shortly afterward, her mother, who lived in the Midwest, died, and Ann drove to her mother's home. On the return trip Ann decided to invest in quilts in memory of her mother. She purchased several quilts and quilt tops on the way home. Now whenever her "farm check" arrives (from her mother's estate) she uses it to add quilts to her collection. Ann's husband says her farm check goes farther than the Federal Budget. Her collection includes a broad range of colors and patterns. Her favorites are red, or red and green quilts, and in particular

appliquéd flowers. She feels she is fortunate to have the shop, as many quilters and collectors bring their quilts in to visually share them with Ann. She has no garage-sale or thrift shop quilts in her collection, but she does love "funky scrap quilts"; perhaps because she identifies with the workmanship—her piecing is never perfect. Ann made her first quilts in the 1960s. She would like someday to have the time to do a floral appliquéd masterpiece with every stitch her own. Until then, she will be content to collect other quiltmaker's work.

SHARON EVANS YENTER

Quilt Collector

Sharon Evans Yenter has been actively involved in quilt collecting since 1975. As the shop owner of In the Beginning—Quilts, she has an opportunity to meet people who have quilts to sell. If it is a family quilt, she tries to convince the people to keep the quilt. Sharon suggests that they record the history of their quilt and document it with pictures, letters, and mementos for future generations. Sharon has two family quilts to pass on to her boys: a Drunkard's Path and a Grandmother's Flower Garden. Her oldest son Jason is a quiltmaker and her younger son Ben loves the older quilts in his mother's collection.

"I have a very eclectic collection," says Sharon. Sometimes a special fabric or a whimsical arrangement appeals to her. She has some spectacular quilts of exceptional workmanship and some that are not examples of superb needlework, but were probably the best the quiltmaker could do. These latter quilts remind Sharon of a passage from *The Velveteen Rabbit*.

Generally, by the time you are Real, most of your hair has been loved off and your eyes drop out and you get loose in the joints and very shabby. But these things don't matter at all, because once you are Real you can't be ugly except to people who don't understand.

This collection has marvelous examples of women's "best quilts," and the quilts that were made to be used daily. It is a tribute to all women who used the needle to keep their family warm and to celebrate special occasions.

MUSEUMS

The following Washington State museums responded to questionnaires requesting information about quilts in their collections. Many of the museums have short hours and are open only during the summer months. If traveling to see quilts, write, enclosing a stamped self-addressed envelope requesting museum hours and the number of quilts currently on display. Asterisks(*) indicate museums that have quilts as part of a permanent display.

Bainbridge Island Historical Museum*
Strawberry Hill Park
P.O. Box 11653
Winslow, WA 98110
(206) 842-4164
(1 quilt)

Benton County Museum and
   Historical Society*
P.O. Box 591
Seventh and Paterson
Prosser, WA 99350
(509) 786-3842
(16 quilts)

Black Diamond Depot Museum*
P.O. Box 232
32627 Railroad Avenue
Black Diamond, WA 98010
(206) 886-1168
(2 quilts)

Blackman Museum*
P.O. Box 174
118 Avenue B
Snohomish, WA 98290
(206) 568-5235
(1 quilt)

Bruce Memorial Museum,
   Waitsburg Historical Society*
P.O. Box 277
318 Main Street
Waitsburg, WA 99361
(509) 337-6688
(12 quilts)

Chelan County Historical Museum*
P.O. Box 22
600 Cottage Avenue
Cashmere, WA 98815
(509) 782-3230
(20 quilts)

Clark County Historical Museum*
1511 Main Street
Vancouver, WA 98660
(206) 695-4681
(19 quilts)

Cowlitz County Historical Museum*
405 Allen Street
Kelso, WA 98626
(206) 577-3119
(24 quilts)

D. O. Pearson Museum*
Box 69
Stanwood Area Historical Society
Stanwood, WA 98292
(206) 629-2072
(4 quilts)

East Benton County Historical
   Society Museum*
P.O. Box 6718
205 Keewaydin Drive
Kennewick, WA 99336
(509) 582-7704
(12 to 15 quilts)

Edmonds South Snohomish
   County Museum*
P.O. Box 52
118 Fifth Avenue North
Edmonds, WA 98020
(206) 778-1403 or 774-0900
(7 quilts)

Ezra Meeker Mansion
P.O. Box 103
321 East Pioneer Street
Puyallup, WA 98371
(206) 845-1402 or 848-1770
(9 quilts)

Fort Walla Walla Museum Complex
Myra Road
(between Rose Street and
Dallas Military Road)
Walla Walla, WA 99362
(509) 525-7703
(30 quilts)

Franklin County Historical Museum*
P.O. Box 1033
305 North Fourth Street
Pasco, WA 99301
(509) 547-3714
(10 quilts)

Grant County Museum*
P.O. Box 1141
742 Basin Street North
Ephrata, WA 98823
(509) 754-3334
(20 quilts)

Greater Maple Valley Historical Museum
P.O. Box 123
Tahoma Administration Building
   (top floor)
23015 Southeast 216th Way
Maple Valley, WA 98038
(206) 255-7588
(4 quilts)

Henry Art Gallery
15th N.E. and N.E. 41st
University of Washington, DE-15
Seattle, WA 98195
(206) 543-2281 or 543-1739
(16 quilts)

Ilwaco Heritage Museum*
P.O. Box 153
115 Southeast Lake
Ilwaco, WA 98624
(206) 642-3446
(10 quilts)

Jefferson County Historical
   Society Museum*
City Hall, 210 Madison
Port Townsend, WA 98368
(206) 385-1003
(3 quilts)

Lewis County Historical Museum*
599 Northwest Front Street
Chehalis, WA 98532
(206) 748-0831
(16 quilts)

Lincoln County Historical Museum*
P.O. Box 585
Sixth and Park
Davenport, WA 99122
(509) 725-0561 or 725-6711
(18 quilts)

Lopez Island Historical Museum
P.O. Box 163
Lopez Village
Weeks and Washburne
Lopez Island, WA 98261
(206) 468-3447 or 468-2049
(15 quilts)

Marymoor Museum*
P.O. Box 162
6846 Lake Sammamish Parkway
Redmond, WA 98073
(206) 885-3684
(60 quilts)

Mukilteo Historical Society Museum*
P.O. Box 166
Third and Lincoln
Mukilteo, WA 98275
(206) 347-5381
(1 quilt)

Museum of History and Industry
2700 24th Avenue East
Seattle, WA 98112
(206) 324-1125
(29 quilts)

Museum of the Clallam County
 Historical Society
223 East Fourth Street
Port Angeles, WA 98362
(206) 452-7831
(25 quilts)

North Central Washington Museum*
127 South Mission Street
Wenatchee, WA 98801
(509) 662-4728
(17 quilts)

Okanogan County Historical Museum
P.O. Box 1129
1410 North Second
Okanogan, WA 98840
(509) 422-4272
(13 quilts)

Orcas Island Historical Museum*
Box 134
North Beach Road
Eastsound, WA 98245
(206) 376-4849
(5 quilts)

Pacific County Historical
 Society Museum*
P.O. Box P
1008 West Robert Bush Drive
South Bend, WA 98586
(206) 875-5224
(5 quilts)

Paul H. Karshner Memorial Museum
309 Fourth Avenue North
Puyallup, WA 98372
(206) 841-8748
(1 quilt)

Pioneer Farm Museum*
The D.O.V.E. Center
1216 Fourth South
Eatonville, WA 98328
(509) 832-6300
(8 quilts)

Polson Park and Museum,
 Historical Society*
P.O. Box 432
1611 Riverside Avenue
Hoquiam, WA 98550
(206) 533-5862
(15 quilts)

Renton Historical Society and Museum
235 Mill Avenue South
Renton, WA 98055
(206) 255-2330
(2 quilts)

San Juan Historical Museum*
P.O. Box 441
405 Prince Street
Friday Harbor, WA 98250
(206) 378-4578
(25 quilts)

Seattle Art Museum
Volunteer Park
14th Avenue East and East Prospect
Seattle, WA 98112
(206) 625-8940
(3 quilts)

Skagit County Historical Museum*
P.O. Box 818
501 South Fourth Street
La Conner, WA 98257
(206) 466-3365
(50 quilts)

Skamania County Historical
 Society Museum
P.O. Box 396
Second Avenue and Vancouver Street
Stevenson, WA 98648
(509) 427-5141
(5 quilts)

Snoqualmie Valley Historical Museum*
P.O. Box 179
320 South North Bend Boulevard
North Bend, WA 98045
(206) 888-3200
(13 quilts)

Stanwood Area Historical Society*
Box 69
27112 102nd Avenue Northwest
Stanwood, WA 98292
(206) 629-2072
(4 quilts)

Sumner Ryan House Museum*
P.O. Box 517
1228 Main Street
Sumner, WA 98390
(206) 863-8936
(6 quilts)

Tacoma Art Museum*
12th and Pacific Avenue
Tacoma, WA 98402
(206) 272-4258
(2 quilts)

Toppenish Museum*
1 South Elm
Toppenish, WA 98948
(509) 865-4510
(4 quilts)

Warden Historical Society Museum*
829 South Steele Road
Othello, WA 99344
(509) 488-2109
(4 quilts)

Washington State Capital Museum
211 West 21st Avenue
Olympia, WA 98501
(206) 753-2580
(30 quilts)

Whatcom Museum of History and Art
121 Prospect Street
Bellingham, WA 98225
(206) 676-6981
(62 quilts)

Wing Luke Asian Museum
407 Seventh Avenue South
Seattle, WA 98104
(206) 623-5124
(1 quilt)

Yakima Valley Museum and
 Historical Association
2105 Tieton Drive
Yakima, WA 98902
(509) 248-0747
(35 quilts)

SELECTED BIBLIOGRAPHY

American Association of University Women. *Women of Washington.* American Association of University Women, Washington State Division, 1977.

Bank, Mirra. *Anonymous Was a Woman.* New York: St. Martins Press, 1979.

Bishop, Robert. *New Discoveries in American Quilts.* New York: E. P. Dutton, 1975.

Bresenhan, Karoline Patterson, and Nancy O'Bryant Puentes. *Lone Stars: A Legacy of Texas Quilts. 1836–1936.* Austin: University of Texas Press, 1986.

Bullard, Lacy Folmar, and Betty Jo Shiell. *Chintz Quilts: Unfading Glory.* Tallahassee, Fla: Serendipity Publishers, 1983.

Clabburn, Pamela. *The Needleworker's Dictionary.* New York: William Morrow, 1976.

Colby, Averil. *Patchwork.* New York: B. T. Batsford, 1958.

——. *Quilting.* New York: Charles Scribner's Sons, 1971.

Drury, Clifford Merrill. *Marcus Whitman, M.D., Pioneer and Martyr.* Caldwell, Idaho: Caxton Printers, 1937.

——. *First White Women Over the Rockies.* Vol. II, *Mrs. Elkanah Walker and Mrs. Cushing Eells.* Glendale, Calif.: Arthur H. Clark, 1963.

Finley, Ruth E. *Old Patchwork Quilts and the Women Who Made Them.* Newton Centre, Mass.: Charles T. Branford, 1970.

Fox, Sandi. *Small Endearments, Nineteenth-Century Quilts for Children.* New York: Charles Scribner's Sons, 1985.

Hall, Carrie A., and Rose G. Kretsinger. *The Romance of the Patchwork Quilt in America.* New York: Bonanza Books, 1935.

Holmes, Kenneth L., ed. *Covered Wagon Women: Diaries and Letters from the Western Trails, 1840–1890.* Glendale, Calif.: Arthur H. Clark, 1983.

Holstein, Jonathan. *The Pieced Quilt, An American Design Tradition.* Boston: New York Graphic Society, 1973.

Ickis, Marguerite. *The Standard Book of Quilt Making and Collecting.* New York: Dover Publications, 1959.

Katzenberg, Dena S. *Baltimore Album Quilts.* Baltimore: The Baltimore Museum of Art, 1981.

Kentucky Quilt Project. *Kentucky Quilts 1800–1900,* Louisville: Kentucky Quilt Project, 1982.

Kolter, Jane Bentley. *Forget Me Not, A Gallery of Friendship and Album Quilts.* Pittstown, New Jersey: Main Street Press, 1985.

Lanansky, Jeannette. *Pieced by Mother, Over 100 Years of Quiltmaking Traditions,* Lewisburg, Penn.: Oral Traditions Project of Union County Historical Society, 1987.

McKim, Ruby Short. *One Hundred and One Patchwork Patterns.* New York: Dover Publications, 1962.

McMorris, Penny. *Crazy Quilts,* New York: E. P. Dutton, 1984.

Mainardi, Patricia. *Quilts, The Great American Art.* San Pedro, Calif.: Miles and Weir, 1978.

Martin, Nancy. *Pieces of the Past.* Bothell, Wash.: That Patchwork Place, 1987.

Meany, Edmond S. *Origin of Washington Geographic Names.* Seattle: University of Washington Press, 1923.

Montgomery, Florence M. *Printed Textiles: English and American Cottons and Linens 1700–1850.* New York: The Viking Press, 1970.

Nelson, Cyril I., and Carter Houck. *Treasury of American Quilts.* New York: Greenwich House, nd (1982).

Orlofsky, Patsy, and Myron Orlofsky. *Quilts in America.* New York: McGraw-Hill, 1974.

Pettit, Florence H. *America's Printed and Painted Fabrics: 1600–1900.* New York: Hastings House, 1970.

Phillips, James W. *Washington State Place Names.* Seattle and London: University of Washington Press, 1971.

Safford, Carleton L., and Robert Bishop. *America's Quilts and Coverlets.* New York: E. P. Dutton, 1972.

Swan, Susan Burrows. *Plain and Fancy: American Women and Their Needlework 1700–1850.* New York: Holt, Rinehart and Winston, 1977.

Told by the Pioneers, Reminiscences of Pioneer Life in Washington. Printed under a project directed by Secretary of State, E. N. Hutchinson, 1937.

Whitney, Marci. *Notable Women.* Tacoma, Wash.; Tacoma News Tribune, 1977.

INDEX

THAT PATCHWORK PLACE
PUBLICATIONS

Baby Quilts From Grandma by Carolann Palmer
Back To Square One by Nancy J. Martin
Branching Out – Tree Quilts by Carolann Palmer
Cathedral Window – A New View by Mary Ryder Kline
Christmas Classics by Sue Saltkill
Christmas Memories – A Folk Art Celebration
    by Nancy J. Martin
Copy Art for Quilters by Nancy J. Martin
Dozen Variables by Marsha McCloskey and
    Nancy J. Martin
Feathered Star Quilts by Marsha McCloskey
Feathered Star Sampler by Marsha McCloskey
Happy Endings – Finishing the Edges of Your Quilt
    by Mimi Dietrich
Holiday Happenings by Christal Carter
Housing Projects by Nancy J. Martin

Little by Little: Quilts in Miniature by Mary Hickey
Make a Medallion by Kathy Cook
More Template-Free Quiltmaking by Trudie Hughes
My Mother's Quilts: Designs from the Thirties
    by Sara Nephew
Pieces of the Past by Nancy J. Martin
Projects for Blocks and Borders by Marsha McCloskey
Quilter's Christmas by Nancyann Twelker
Quilts From a Different Angle by Sara Nephew
Small Quilts by Marsha McCloskey
Template-Free Quiltmaking by Trudie Hughes
Wall Quilts by Marsha McCloskey

For more information, send $2 for color catalog to That Patchwork Place, Inc., P.O. Box 118, Bothell, WA 98041-0118. Many titles available at your local quilt shop.

Quilting bee, 1930s. Mary Cora Courtney (center front). (Courtesy Carole Fletcher, Vashon Island)

�֍ A special thank you to the patrons and sponsors who generously supported "Women and Their Quilts: A Washington State Centennial Tribute" traveling quilt show.

PATRONS

Quilters Anonymous
In The Beginning Quilts
That Patchwork Place, Inc.
Dicmar Publications
Omnigrid, Inc.
Quilts Northwest

DONORS

I.R.B.Q. Quilt Club
Block Party Quilters
Fidalgo Island Quilters
Martha Lake Sew & Sews
Martha Lake Community Club
Mr. & Mrs. Petter Johanson
Ann Louise Fabric & Folkart
Wednesday Friendship Quilters
The Comforters
Contemporary Quilt Association
Port Orchard Quilter's Guild
Busy Bee Quilters
Northwest Quilting Connection
Kitsap Quilters
Northwest Quilters, Inc.
Clark County Quilters
Spokane Valley Quilters
Putnam Batting Company, Inc.
V.I.P. Fabrics
American Quilters Society
Swiss Metrosene, Inc.
Evergreen Quilters Guild
Narrows Connection Quiltmakers
Fabric Sales Company
Hoffman California Fabrics
Stearns and Foster Company
Quilter's Newsletter Magazine

WOMEN AND THEIR QUILTS COMMITTEE MEMBERS

NANCYANN TWELKER
Chairman and Curator

GERRY BOURSSE
Secretary-Treasurer

NANCY J. MARTIN
Publications

ROSALIE PFEIFER
Exhibits

JANET LOCKHART
Fundraising

DE LORIS STUDE
West Coast Quilter's Conference

ANN STOHL
Ann Louise Fabric and Folkart

VICKIE MCKENNEY
Calico Basket

SHARON YENTER
In the Beginning—Quilts

CATHY MITCHELL
Quilts Northwest Ltd.

DONNA EINES

NANCY JOHNSON

JOYCE PENNINGTON